Dear Bookseller,

The last time we were this excited about a business parable was when the original agent for Ken Blanchard and Spencer Johnson sent Hyperion the manuscript for FISH!, which has gone on to sell 1.5 million hardcover copies to date. Now, this same agent has sent us KINGDOMALITY, a parable unlike any you have seen before and one we are convinced will forever change the way people practice and even talk about the art of management.

Kingdomality is an extraordinarily accurate method of determining your own and your employees' strengths and weaknesses. By taking a simple, eight-question test online at Kingdomality.com, you can determine which of twelve different roles you would have played in a medieval kingdom (or you can take the test right in this book and find which of four general groups you'd belong to)—and how each role is essential in the running of a medieval kingdom—or any business anywhere.

More than 12 million people have already taken the Kingdomality test online and they will all be receiving an e-mail blast on publication day urging them to go to their bookstores to buy this book. Give the test a try—it takes less than five minutes—and you will see why there is so much excitement about KINGDOMALITY.

Let us know what you think—and who you are!

Sincerely,

Will Schwalbe
Dreamer-Minstrel

KINGDOMALITY

KINGDOMALITY

*An Ingenious New Way to
Triumph in Management*

SHELDON BOWLES

RICHARD SILVANO

SUSAN SILVANO

HYPERION NEW YORK

Library of Congress Cataloging-in-Publication Data

Bowles, Sheldon M.
    Kingdomality : an ingenious new way to triumph in management / Sheldon Bowles, Susan Silvano, Richard Silvano.
        p.   cm.
    ISBN 1-4013-0135-5
    1. Management.   2. Executive ability.   3. Teams in the workplace.
4. Personality.   I. Silvano, Susan   II. Silvano, Richard   III. Title.
HD31.B713 2005
658.4—dc22

                                        2004040624

Hyperion books are available at special quantity discounts to use as premiums or for special programs, including corporate training. For details contact Michael Rentas, Manager, Inventory and Premium Sales, Hyperion, 77 West 66th Street, 11th floor, New York, New York 10023, or call 212-456-0133.

FIRST EDITION

10 9 8 7 6 5 4 3 2 1

Dedication TK

FOREWORD

$\mathcal{B}$Y NATURE, BY INSTINCT, by personality, people react differently and use different techniques and ways of dealing with a situation. Success in the future will come to those who see people as unique individuals with unique talents. Rather than just selecting people with the right skills, winning organizations will focus on selecting people with the right skills who are *also* suited by temperament to successfully complete the task.

How do you discover who you really are? Who your team members really are? What role you're best adapted to play? Many systems have been devised based on the teachings of the great psychologist-psychiatrist Carl Jung. The best may well be a system called Kingdomality, created by Richard and Susan Silvano of Career Management International. Kingdomality links an understanding of personality—the natural/instinctive way we act and react—with role models that clearly define the whole sweep of personality types.

By matching personality types to roles played by citizens in a medieval kingdom and developing a simple test that is blind to issues such as gender, race, education, economic circumstance, and so forth, the Silvanos have created a way of discovering who you are. By knowing your own role, and the essence of other roles, you'll understand why certain people see problems and opportunities differently. Kingdomality also helps you identify your own strengths and blind spots as well as those of others.

Kingdomality teaches three lessons I love. First, the Kingdom can't function properly unless all points of view are present. Everyone is needed. Second, although different issues at different times may best be served by a certain type of individual, inherently all are of equal value. Third, no one role is best suited to being leader.

Anyone can take the lead. Anyone, that is, who understands his or her own strengths and the strengths of others. And Kingdomality teaches exactly that.

To know who you truly are is an understanding that brings power and mastery to your life. To know who your coworkers are and to understand what they are thinking and why they are thinking that way makes for far more effective and powerful partnerships.

Kingdomality the book is a fun, easy-to-read story filled with insights and information that will make a difference to you both at work and at home. But, before you start to read, I urge you to visit *www.kingdomality.com* and join the more than six million people who have already discovered what role they'd best fulfill in Kingdomality's medieval kingdom.

I am a Kingdomality Dreamer-Minstrel, as is my friend and colleague Sheldon Bowles, the Silvanos co-author. Richard Silvano is a Discoverer and Susan a Prime Minister. What does that all mean? Well, visit the Internet, find out who you are, and then read on!

Ken Blanchard

NOTE TO READERS

*B*EFORE YOU READ *Kingdomality*, we urge you to find an Internet connection and take the short, multiple-question test you'll find at *www.kingdomality .com*, which will determine your personality type and peg which of twelve roles you would have filled in a medieval kingdom.

If you can't access the Web right now, then turn to the end of this book where on page 00 you'll find the Create a Country test. It's an easy, eight-question, multiple-choice test. Without the Kingdomality Web site to calculate test results, you won't be able to pinpoint your role, but you will be able to determine which guildhall you belong to. There are four guildhalls: (1) Explorers, (2) Maintainers, (3) Helpers', and (4) Challengers'. All Kingdomality roles fit within one of the four guildalls.

Knowing your role, or which guildhall you belong to, will make reading *Kingdomality* more fun and interesting. So, please go to page 00 or to *www.kingdomality.com* now. Enjoy!

CHAPTER ONE

WE MEET KING HAROLD

ONCE UPON A TIME, and in a land far away, there lived a King, Harold the Wise, in the midst of chaos. We say the King was wise only because all Kings, country or corporate, are said to be wise. It's one of the advantages of being Royal. Even the biggest jerks, if also Royal, are said to be gracious, witty, and wise. A couple of examples, again both country and corporate, may well pop into mind.

Now, our King was a nice enough chap, and he certainly wasn't a dolt. But, if he had been really wise, he would have checked the real estate ads, "Orderly,

Well-Kept Countries Available," in *The Royal Review,* the leading journal of its day for Royal personages, to find a better-ordered Kingdom, with easier subjects to govern.

Unfortunately in *his* Kingdom, projects got started but were rarely finished. Meetings called to discuss *how* to get a project concluded would soon turn into meetings discussing *why* the project wasn't completed, which in reality meant everybody disclaimed any responsibility for the mess and blamed everyone else. King Harold's Court Jester once spent two weeks in the town square stocks after nailing the following poster on the door of the Royal Palace:

THE FIVE PHASES OF A PROJECT

- Enthusiasm
- Trouble
- Search for a Scapegoat
- Punishment of the Innocent
- Praise and Reward for All Nonparticipants

The Kingdom didn't run well because the people didn't run well. By that we mean they were, for the most part, grumpy, out-of-sorts, quarrelsome, and defeatist. The only people who got along were like-minded individuals who banded together. They resembled bands of chattering monkeys, which, when trouble strikes, head for the treetops, scolding whoever and whatever is left below. Ofttimes King Harold's subjects weren't exactly sure what they were squabbling about, but still they battled.

So, there you have it: a Kingdom with poor productivity and unhappy, unreliable, and unfulfilled subjects banding together with friends and turning on, rather than working with, each other. In short, a situation much like many modern-day organizations.

While our King wasn't as wise as he might have been, he also wasn't anybody's fool. He knew the Kingdom was a mess and he knew the reason wasn't a lack of resources, lack of Royal support for new initiatives, lack of training, or lack of capital from the Royal Treasury—all of which were frequently cited by citizens seeking to assign blame for the Kingdom's troubles.

The real problem was a people problem. The King would come up with an exciting new program, explain it fully and carefully to all, assign responsibility, and command everyone to give it their best. Their best, or at least what they called their best, was usually disaster. People just didn't perform. Unless you counted bickering and backbiting as performance. When caught out for nonperformance, they adopted the BLAM system of damage control: Blame, Lie, And Misrepresent.

The King had tried floggings, prison, banishment, and beheadings. Nothing worked. Then a well-meaning, itinerant management consultant said the problem was that King Harold was punishing his subjects, not rewarding them. Soon dozens of awards, totaling ten pounds of gold from the Royal Treasury, had been handed out. Yet the citizens messed up as badly as ever. Even those given the gold!

The management consultant had the theory down, but he turned out to be short on the implementation side. Trouble was, in part, that the King was rewarding people for doing the wrong things, and so they just kept on doing the wrong things, only now more often! The other part of the King's trouble was that he still hadn't fixed his core problem: unhappy, out-of-sorts, grumbling, and grumpy people. Every time one person was rewarded, hundreds of others who weren't went into a blue funk and complained loudly and vociferously about how unfair the reward system was. The consultant's advice wasn't working.

Having burned clients before with theory, and no "go" in the make-it-happen department, the itinerant management consultant knew when to move on. He cleared the castle gate just in time. A fast horse and cloudy night saved him from a date with the King's favorite flogger.

Again, there you have it. Nonperforming people. Ever-increasing levels of punishment that didn't improve performance. Misdirected rewards that made matters worse. A management consultant who was not up to the challenge. In short, the problems faced by our King were very much like those faced by many modern managers.

One day, not long after the Jester had been released from the stocks and the management consultant had successfully fled the Kingdom, a particularly potent wizard showed up at the Palace door seeking an audience with the King.

"I'm here to grant you one wish," said the Wizard. "The Supreme Wizard has sent me out to visit the four corners of the world and grant a wish to every Kingdom. It's all part of the Supreme Wizard's 750th Wedding Anniversary Celebration."

King Harold looked at the Wizard suspiciously. This might be a powerful wizard facing the King, all decked out in a brilliant Emerald Green robe and with a very proper pointed wizard's hat with floppy brim, but as we've told you already, our King, while perhaps no genius, was no fool. It was well known, in the time of which we speak, that traveling wizards would come by every hundred years or so, and if sent out to grant *three* wishes, were perfectly capable of secreting *two* for their own use—that is, if they could get away with awarding only one.

"I thought wizards granted three wishes," challenged the King.

"You should meet the Supreme Wizard's wife," said the Wizard by way of explanation. "This is a one-wish wife! Matter of fact, the Supreme Wizard isn't such a great catch either. Definitely a one-wish Supreme Wizard, if you ask me. I can swear on a pickled lizard I don't have *three* wishes to grant."

As everyone knows, or at least as everyone knew then, no oath was more solemn to a wizard than one made over a pickled lizard. Accordingly, our King, noting both the Wizard's sincerity and offer of a pickled-lizard oath, accepted the one-wish offer. This left for the Wizard's own use one of the two wishes he'd been sent out with. Our King was dealing with an experienced wizard who had previously visited eighteen kingdoms and was so far batting twelve out of eighteen when it came to holding on to the second wish.

One wish was all the King needed, though. He made good use of it. In his later years the King grudgingly admitted, when pressed, that if it hadn't been for the Court Jester's poster, and the incident with the well-meaning management consultant, he might well have wished for a new palace or a victory at that year's Royal Jousting Festival. However, his mind was much on the way his Kingdom functioned, or rather, didn't function.

"Well, Wizard," said the King, "my Kingdom is a mess. Nothing runs very well and my people aren't happy. I'd like you to fix that."

A pained look came over the Wizard's face. Kingdom correction took time. "I've got some magnificent jewels. A magic harp that will play perfect music whenever you want. I've even got some very lovely Royal brides," he added with a meaningful look at the King, for the bachelorhood of King Harold's eldest son at the ripe old age of twenty was a source of angst to the King.

The King wasn't to be distracted. "Fix the problem. Or aren't you powerful enough?"

The Wizard winced. "Not powerful enough! Kingdom correction is a piece of cake for a particularly potent wizard such as myself. Just don't come back to me next year and complain that you should have gone for the jewels or a bride for your son."

"No complaints," said the King. "Promise."

The Wizard gave a shrug and tilted his head as if to say "It's on your head, not mine."

"Do you have to cast a spell or something?" asked the King.

"Could if you want me to," said the Wizard. "I can wave my wand. Poofs of smoke can be impressive. Chants are always nice. At home I have a cauldron and do a nice potion. But I'm a fifth-degree wizard. I'm not just starting out. At my stage it's all show. Not actually necessary."

"So what's next?" asked the King.

"Next is Lady Elizabeth of Whimble, Freeman, and Frost. She should be here any minute."

"Whimble, Freeman, and Frost?" puzzled the King.

"Best management consultants available," said the Wizard. "Lady Elizabeth specializes in people issues. You've got a people problem."

At the words "management consultants," the King, who remembered very well the ten pounds of gold the last one had cost his Royal Treasury, began to rise up off his throne.

His bellow of protest was cut off in mid-roar by the sudden appearance of a woman beside the Wizard.

"Ah! Lady Elizabeth," said the Wizard. "King Harold was just about to tell me his thoughts on management consultants."

The King, being a very proper sort of Royal personage and easily distracted by the ladies, ignored the Wizard's comment. "Lady Elizabeth. How nice to meet you."

"Likewise, I'm sure, Your Highness," she said. "Sorry

I was delayed. I wanted to take a quick tour of your Kingdom before I met with you."

"A tour? But we just called for you now," said the King.

"I'm a bit of a wizard myself," said Lady Elizabeth with a smile. "I whipped around the whole thing in less than fifteen seconds."

"That won't be what her time sheet says, I bet," said the Wizard with a knowing look at the King.

Lady Elizabeth looked down at the Wizard, for she was close to six feet tall and the Wizard, like most wizards of the day, was, at best, four foot five.

"Don't pay him any attention," she said to the King. "He's just jealous. He's tried three times to get his wizard-consulting papers. Hasn't made it yet!"

If looks could kill, Lady Elizabeth would have been finished by the Wizard's glare. She, however, wasn't about to be put off by a furious wizard, particularly potent or not. Besides, she was angry. Her time sheet already showed three days of investigative work checking out the Kingdom, and now, she knew, she'd have to correct the "error."

Lady Elizabeth's discomfort was no match for the Wizard's anger, which became even more acute when he stomped his foot and disappeared in a puff of smoke. No one seemed to notice, or care.

"As I was saying," she said politely to the King, "I've checked out the Kingdom and you have what in management literature is referred to as the east-west-north-south-square-peg-in-a-round-hole problem."

"Which is?" prompted the King.

"Which is a fancy way of saying that the people are confused about who they really are, and you keep trying to make these confused people do things and behave in ways they're not suited to do. It's like asking a musician to juggle."

The King had heard the diagnosis waltz sung by management consultants before. He was wary. He was also interested, so he gave Lady Elizabeth a smile of encouragement and she continued.

"Your east-west-north-south problem comes first. If you don't know your people, you don't know anything! What works with one isn't productive with another."

Management out of touch with the workers? Sound familiar? Read on! But, if in your organization you think management is in touch with who the workers really are, then it's time to pick up a different book. And do please give the authors a call. We've got a great bridge to sell you. And for you it's a deal![1]

---

[1]Our esteemed editorial adviser, Michal Yanson, on whom we depend for guidance on many matters, has warned us that this is insulting to managers, that not all managers are out of touch, and that we should tone this down. With concern and trepidation we let it stand. An author seeking success ignores Ms. Yanson's advice at their peril. However, we feel a tough-worded overstatement is a necessary wake-up call for many, and we apologize for so unfairly including you in our sweeping statement.

CHAPTER TWO

THE FOUR CORNERS
OF THE KINGDOM

*T*HE KING FOUND IT easy to accept that what worked with one person wouldn't work with another. But that alone wasn't very helpful. He needed more. "So, who are these people? What have I got?"

"Four main groups. Every Kingdom has four main groups. Often located in their own place. They like to hang out together," replied Lady Elizabeth.

"Let's start with your southerners. Nice folk. Mostly laid back, generally easy to get along with. But when they get wrapped up in an issue, they're passionate. Hot-blooded southerners. They love a cause. Not always practical. Some are wild-eyed idealists. They love to help others and appreciate recognition for their efforts. Emotions rule the way they relate to the world. We call them *Helpers.*

"In the north you've got cooler folk. More rational. More efficient. More logical. To them, being better, *doing* better, getting better makes sense, and so they like to set goals and push the limits. You're not going to get away with fuzzy thinking with these folk. They'll challenge any thought, anything or anybody who stands between them and success. Because this challenge is so logical to them, they are often unaware of the impact their questioning can have on others, who can see them as rude and even abusive. They're master strategists, and logic rules the way they relate to the world. They're the *Challengers.*

"Opposite ends of the Kingdom and quite opposite in the way they see the world. And, of course, the way they see the world dictates how they deal with the world."

"Good call," said the King. "My subjects down south would rather siesta than work, unless, of course, they've got a bee in their bonnet. Then they can mount a crusade on a moment's notice. Trouble is, the crusade will be to right a wrong or establish some principle or other. No booty for the Royal Treasury! Helpers is a good name for them.

"Up north it's the opposite, all right. If they can't get a slice of some treasure, or something they want, they won't crusade. I issue a proclamation announcing a new crusade, and if there's no payoff for them, they swamp me with objections. They're loyal if they believe the crusade makes sense. They're not rebellious, but they sure are an argumentative, cantankerous lot. They're Challengers, all right. They're always making plans, training for success, and demanding the rest of the Kingdom 'get with the program.'"

"Well then," said Lady Elizabeth, "how about the next group. The westerners. 'Nuff said! These are the pushers of the envelope. Always seeking new experiences. They like unusual houses and want to cook over a fire outside. They claim the food tastes better with a little dirt on it. Weird hairdos, strange new religions, backpacking with a tent, and creating the fad-of-the-day keeps them busy. Nothing they like better than trying something or someplace new. Chaos doesn't frighten these people. Many of them see past lives, future lives, and parallel lives, all at the same time. These are the visionaries of the Kingdom. Their creativity dictates how they relate to the world. They're called *Explorers*.

"The easterners are opposite in geography and temperament. Stuffed shirts, some say. Their idea of casual Friday is a beige, instead of a white, ruffled collar. While the rest of the Kingdom is off helping, challenging, and exploring, these are the people who keep the home fires burning, the supply lines to the north, south, and west open, and the Kingdom functioning. They're dependable. They love to see everything running properly. New is a stressful word. Change isn't a good idea. They know innovation invites glitches, so they avoid anything untried or untested. As for home life, not only do they cook in the kitchen, they insist on sitting up at the table to eat.

"'If it was good enough for grandpa, it's good enough for me,' marks the way they think. Life is serious business. Many of them think the rest of the Kingdom is as mad as a March Hare. Those 'March Hares' often see easterners as fussbudgets and stick-in-the-muds. The fact is, however, they keep the Kingdom running. They know life is a train going down a track and someone has to keep it on the rails. And chances are it's a supply train. Easterners love to be sure everything and everybody is well supplied and everything is in order. That's their job. They're the realists of the Kingdom and being realistic is how these easterners deal with the world. These folk are the *Maintainers*."

"That's my Kingdom," said King Harold. "The subjects out west like to go crusading so much they go off on their own! Just to see what's over the mountain. When I go out there on a Royal Visit they honor me with a cookout and folk songs. In the east I get a formal meal in some huge dining hall and two hours of speeches. You're right about easterners and supply trains. If an easterner goes to war, you'll find him or her in the supply department. Matter of fact, the only time an easterner gets killed on a crusade is if the supply wagon turns over. That is, if he or she goes at all. Ofttimes they're too busy taking a census or writing up my Royal Proclamations to go anywhere. Frankly, I think those are just excuses. Truth is, easterners don't like to leave home to gad about.

"But, be that as it may, it sounds like a good balance. East balances west. North and south. All bases covered. What's the problem?" asked the King.

"Three problems. First, most all the Helpers, Challengers, Explorers, and Maintainers live in their own part of the Kingdom. 'Birds of a feather' and all that. You've got the bases covered, but the balance isn't really there. And you need balance if you're going to have a healthy, productive Kingdom. No one person, no one role is more important than another. Everybody is needed, each doing his or her thing, alongside each other, not off with a bunch of similar people who think and act just like they do."

The parallel to teams in present-day organizations is, we think, obvious. Too often teams are balanced for such things as business and technical skills but not for outlook and approach. Squeaky wheels get greased, all right—right off the team. Like-minded is equated with right-thinking. Like-minded, though, can easily lead to stuck-in-a-rut thinking, not right-thinking. Which leads us to the second problem Lady Elizabeth was about to name:

"Second, they fight. Your subjects don't understand people who think differently, approach a problem differently. They don't value a contrary opinion. They fight it as heresy, rather than another window on truth.

"Third, you've got some really mixed-up people. They not only don't understand others, they don't understand themselves. Helpers who think they ought to be Explorers, Challengers focused on being Maintainers, Maintainers desperately trying to be Helpers, and so on down the line. It's a mess!"

"So why do they do that?" asked the King in a puzzled tone of voice. "Try to be someone or something they're not?"

"Good question," replied Lady Elizabeth. "People get it into their heads, or more likely a parent or teacher plants it there, that they're supposed to be a certain kind of person. Perhaps they hear a story and fall in love with one of the characters and want to be just like that person.

"And you, Your Majesty, you're part of the problem too."

"I'm sure I'm not."

"But you are. You have no idea who people really are either, so you keep asking people to do things that, by their fundamental nature, they're not suited to do. Either from some misguided idea of equality or blind bullheadedness, you assign tasks and have expectations for performance regardless of a person's natural style. People don't work that way. At least they don't if you want optimal performance."

Once again we see things weren't so different, way back then. We'd be filthy rich if we had a dollar for every organization today that assigns tasks based on cookie-cutter thinking, ignoring people's personal styles.

Under most any other circumstance, Lady Elizabeth's crack about "blind bullheadedness," wizard consultant or not, would have earned her two weeks in the stocks, but the King was too intrigued with what she was saying to notice.

"So what do I do? How do I fix this?" asked the King.

"It's called Kingdomality," replied Lady Elizabeth. "It's matching the needs of the Kingdom to each person's individual personality. By personality I mean who the person really is. To know who each one really is, you need to know how he or she instinctively reacts to situations, what their fundamental nature is. This, in turn, dictates how they relate to the world and to others."

The King looked thoughtful, then interested, and

moments later a smile burst over his face. "Square-peg-in-a-round-hole! What you're saying is that I've been assigning inappropriate tasks to people not because the tasks are bad, but because the people aren't suited to the task. They might have the necessary skills, but if the work isn't a natural fit, they won't be productive."

"That's it. You wouldn't dream of appointing a Royal Treasurer who couldn't count. But if all you do is look at number skills, you might give the job to an Explorer. Lots of Explorers would do an excellent job, but depending on what you want accomplished, you might be better off with a Maintainer. The trick is to match not only skills, resources, and incentives to what needs doing, but also the basic personality of the person. Any personality can do any job, and do it well, depending on your definition of 'well' at the time."

"At the time?"

"Of course, at the time," Lady Elizabeth replied. "When things are going well, you want a Royal Treasurer who can keep a close eye on the books and a tight lock on the castle vault. If a war comes along, someone who's good at raising new tax revenue might be best. The kind of person who is happy working in an office with numbers and the one who likes to get out in the field and collect taxes are very different. I'd be looking at a Maintainer for the first job and a Challenger for the second. If I wanted someone to look for creative new ways of taxing, I'd interview Explorers."

"And I haven't been," said the King.

"No, you haven't. And here's another problem. When you need a job done, you usually pick the head person and then let that person go off and choose the people he or she needs."

"I delegate," said the King with obvious pride.

"More like abdicate," said Lady Elizabeth. "Your managers don't understand the need to put together teams that have both the necessary skills and the right balance of personality roles. The result is that Explorers hire Explorers and Maintainers hire Maintainers. Look at your school system. Filled with Maintainer teachers and principals and you wonder why the place is deadly dull, with students assigned times to exercise, times to study, times to be creative. Imagine! Times to be creative. The amazing part is that Maintainer teachers can't even see how bizarre it is—at least how bizarre it is to creative Explorers—to have set times for music and art. Explorers may see forcing children to line up at the school door as silly."

"It *is* a little silly when you think about it, isn't it?" said the King thoughtfully.

"Not if you're a Maintainer. To a Maintainer it's the sanest, most reasonable thing in the world. How else would you keep a ragtag band of children on track? To do otherwise would be loony to a Maintainer. And he or she couldn't even begin to entertain the question an Explorer would ask: Why do they need to be on track in the first place?"

"I'll turn the schools over to Explorers!" the King exclaimed.

"Now there's an idea!" said Lady Elizabeth. "The students will spend half their time on field trips and the other half dancing with poetic elves to expand their conscious level. Not much math, not much reading, but lots of experiences—if, as, and when, of course, the students bother to come. If they don't, the Explorers won't worry. They'll assume the kids are just off getting in touch with their inner selves or whatever."

"Damned if I do, damned if I don't," said the King. "Balance, you're going to tell me. Right?"

"Right. Remember when you put Sir Lockletter in charge of the army and the knights all marched off to do battle in the War of the Sacred Relics?"

The King winced. "Got halfway there and ran out of supplies."

"A few Maintainers could have made a difference," said Lady Elizabeth. "Lockletter was a good choice in many ways. He had a real passion for the cause. He's a member of the Helper group, and his personality role is what we call a White Knight. White Knights are one of the three possible personality roles for helpers. Lockletter's problem was that he gathered around him a whole army of White Knights. Great warriors for the right cause, but not always the most practical of people."

"You can say that again," said the King, shaking his head at the memory of his stranded army. "Defeated before we even started to battle. I was so humiliated it was three years before I was brave enough to show my face again at the Annual Convention of Kings and Queens."

Again we think the parallels to present-day organizations are clear. Much is made in the corporate world, both in profit and not-for-profit organizations, of the need for motivating leaders who inspire workers with a clear vision. A fine thing. However, it doesn't do any good when leaders know what they want and managers are in a quandary as to how to get there. Worse yet is when they, like Sir Lockletter, think they have all bases covered but because of their own limited perspective not only don't see the other bases, they don't even recognize their own view as being too well defined (narrow) to recognize something might be missing!

CHAPTER THREE

KINGDOMALITY'S
TWELVE ROLES

*T*HE REMINDER OF THE Sir Lockletter debacle showed King Harold that while his Kingdom was home to Explorers, Maintainers, Challengers, and Helpers, it wasn't as homogeneous as he'd once thought. He needed to better understand his people, all right, but the implications of that were worrisome.

"I can see how people divide up into four main groups—the Explorers, Maintainers, Challengers, and Helpers. But obviously, that's just a start. How am I ever going to know individual personalities? I've got

387,418 subjects. That's way too many to understand," he said to Lady Elizabeth.

"Then I've got good news. To start, all you need to do is understand which of the four main groups people, and yourself, fit into. Do that and you'll be well on your way to solving most of your problems. Even if that's all you ever do, you'll be a winner. But if you want to take the next step, that's easy. While there are countless variations in your Kingdom, it all boils down to just twelve personality types. Twelve roles. The White Knight role I mentioned is one of those types.

"For now, don't worry about the twelve," said Lady Elizabeth. "Concentrate on the four main groups. Get those, and you've got it. But, with your wish, you're entitled to know about the twelve roles and so I'm going to give you a short introduction. Most people, once they master the four main groups and figure out where they fit in, get excited when they see what a difference it makes and want to take the next step."

"If I can get away with four, I'll stick to four. I'll never keep twelve straight," said King Harold.

"We'll see," said Lady Elizabeth with a smile that suggested her wizard powers could foresee a different future. "But just in case, I'll give you a brief overview. Besides, as I said, it's all paid for. It's included in your wish. Kingdomality kingdom correction includes an introduction to the twelve roles."

"If I've paid, courtesy of the Wizard, of course, I'd best get what I've got coming to me then," said the King, for like all kings, country or corporate, he liked to get what he'd paid for. Then, and again like all kings, he challenged, "Just an introduction?"

"A quick gloss-over," confirmed Lady Elizabeth. "Consultants don't tell you everything on the first visit. Then you wouldn't need to have us back—buy the second book, so to speak."

"Second book?" asked the King.

"Just a figure of speech," she replied.

"The good news is that the twelve are pretty easy to remember," continued Lady Elizabeth. "They all fit together, like the hours on a sundial. Maintainers clustered at three o'clock, Explorers at nine, Challengers at twelve, and Helpers at six. There are three roles in each group—one for each hour on the sundial.

"And here's a bonus: You already know four of them. You just need to learn the role names. The basic Helper is our White Knight. Off to right a wrong, rescue a maiden, do what has to be done. The Challenger archetype is the Black Knight. Black Knights focus on success. Goal set for it. Train for it. Go for it. And they like to get paid. The ultimate Explorer is the Bishop— the professional chameleon who can creatively slide from one side of an issue to another.[1] Visions of other worlds, new experiences, other lifetimes are the Bishop's domain. Maintainer central is run by the Scientist. Chances are you'll find the Scientist in the lab, deep down under the castle. That's a great place for a lab. Winter or summer, rain or shine, day or night, it's all the same down there. Scientific Method is another way of saying Maintainer. Rules and regulations, policies and procedures, tried and true, right way and wrong way, order, order, order. That's your Scientist.

"Remember those four roles, and you're well on your way to mastering Kingdomality."

The King said, "White Knight, Black Knight, Bishop, Scientist. I'll grant you, they're easy enough to remember."

---

[1]Please remember, dear reader, that we speak of roles in a Medieval Kingdom. We don't suggest that this Bishop role necessarily relates to any current or recent holder of that title in any religious persuasion known to us. Oh no! Heaven forbid!

"You'll find all twelve roles are easy to remember. Especially if you plot them out on the face of a sundial. Take a look at this." Lady Elizabeth took a quill pen and parchment and drew:

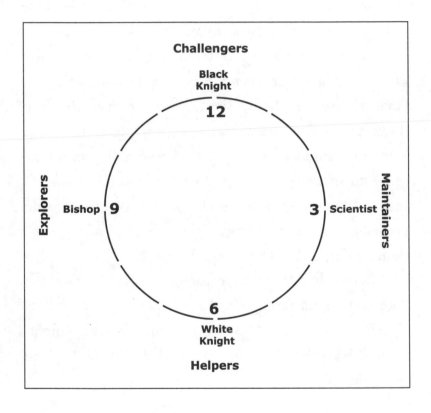

"Kingdomality looks like a great theory, all right. But how do I use it?"

"It *is* great in theory. Even better in application,"

Lady Elizabeth replied. "As for making use of Kingdomality, that comes later. First you need to meet someone. I did some work with King Peter the Blessed about
ten years ago. Perhaps you've heard of him."

The King looked at Lady Elizabeth with new respect.
"You were in on the makeover of *that* Kingdom? Darn
right I've heard of him. We used to call him Peter the
Befuddled. Now his country is running like a charm, and
he won't tell the rest of us what he's doing."

"Kingdomality. That's what he's doing," said Lady
Elizabeth. "I've arranged for you to meet one of his subjects. It will be a good introduction to the Kingdomality
roles. The roles here in your Kingdom are the same as in
Peter's, of course. The difference is that Peter's subjects
understand their roles."

"Peter's guy is coming here?" asked King Harold.

"We're going there," said Lady Elizabeth. "Transportation courtesy of our wizard friend—that is, if he is
still around?"

"Right here," said the Wizard, who appeared, as he
had departed, in a puff of smoke and with enough edge
in his voice to make it clear if anyone cared, which they
didn't, that he was still chuffed.

CHAPTER FOUR

A VISIT WITH ALFRED

TRANSPORTATION VIA wizard express concerned the King, and he was going to say so when he felt a whoosh of air and suddenly found himself sitting on a rock beside a small rural road. One moment he was sitting on his throne, the next on a rural rock. Kings, country or corporate, rarely take kindly to being dispossessed of their thrones, and our King was no exception. Adding to his distress was the realization he was no longer in his own Kingdom. His kingdom was flat. Ahead were mountains!

"What the . . . ," the King started to say but broke

off when he spotted the Wizard and Lady Elizabeth walking toward him. Lady Elizabeth was chewing out the Wizard something fierce.

"I've told you before, we go when I say go. Not a moment before or after."

"The convection was conducive," said the Wizard. "If you weren't ready, don't blame me. After all, you're the one who is *certified*. Of all people I thought *you'd* be ready." Our Wizard, we regret to say, wasn't only particularly potent. He could also be particularly petty.

"What's going on here?" the King demanded.

"We've arrived at the outskirts of Peter's Kingdom," said Lady Elizabeth. "I've brought you here to meet Alfred. He's the leader of Peter's finest troupe of actors, musicians, jugglers, and magicians. The troupe is called the Lords and Ladies. They should be along any moment now."

As if on cue, the raucous sound of band music reached the King's ears and then the musicians appeared around a bend in the road. A tall man, dressed in a bright yellow costume and carrying a long black rod, which he pumped up and down to the music, led the parade.

"The Shepherd has arrived," said Lady Elizabeth as the yellow-clad leader halted right in front of them where, with a final flourish of his rod, he ended the music.

"What Shepherd?" demanded the King.

"That's our Shepherd. Leading the whole shebang! Your Majesty, meet Alfred, leader of Lords and Ladies."

"Delighted to meet you," said Alfred, bowing.

"Damnedest looking Shepherd I've ever seen. No sheep. Wouldn't cut it in my Kingdom," said the King.

"Wrong kind of Shepherd," said Lady Elizabeth. "Shepherd is the name of one of the twelve Kingdomality roles. It's one of the three possible roles for Helpers."

Lady Elizabeth continued. "I've brought you here for three reasons. First, Peter's kingdom is successful because of Kingdomality. Yours can be, too. You just need to understand and work with your subjects' natural talents. Second, Alfred is a Shepherd, and understanding Shepherds is a great place to start to learn about Kingdomality. Third, Alfred is a good example of how role names, and actual employment in the real world, aren't necessarily connected."

"So, a Kingdomality Shepherd doesn't have sheep?" asked the King, looking Alfred up and down.

"He might," answered Alfred. "Shepherds always

like a flock, be it people or sheep," he added with a
wave of his hand toward the Lords and Ladies.

"We Shepherds like to look after people. Tend the
flock. Our primary personality is Helper. We're driven by
emotion, but we're a bit Maintainer as well. Our secondary trait is being realistic. Shepherds think being
emotionally realistic is about as close to perfection as you
can get, but Kingdomality has taught us to value the way
others see things."

"On the sundial face, Shepherds are at five o'clock,"
said Lady Elizabeth as she unrolled the parchment. She
then labeled five o'clock "Shepherd." "I'll also mark in
the essential element of each personality type. Emotional for Helpers, logical for Challengers, realistic for
Maintainers, and creative for Explorers. And it's much
like a map, so I'll show the directions, too."

"Looks good," said the King. "But what is personality? I want to be sure I understand what *you* mean by it."

"Good question. I touched on personality when we
first met, but I'm not surprised you missed it, what with
wizards and consultants showing up. Let me give it to
you again. Personality is the essence of who a person
really is. That means how he or she instinctively reacts,

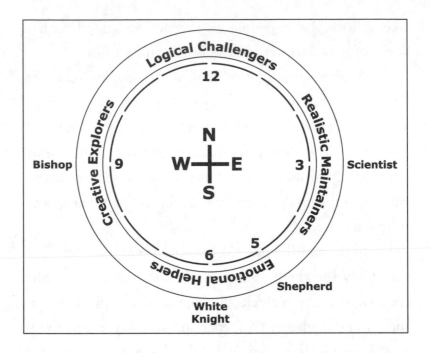

what their fundamental nature is. It shows up fast under stress. Major stress can blow away social graces and control. Our true self shines through. This true self, personality, dictates how we deal with life. We may try to hide it, or pretend it's different than it really is, but it's at the center of our being and it's what drives us," said Lady Elizabeth.

Alfred said, "That's the difference between the four main Kingdomality groups—personality.

"In a crisis Helpers become emotional and seize on a solution that satisfies the heart. The solution might not work, but it will feel good.

"Challengers seek the logical solution. The one that satisfies the brain. It might not please others, but it's bound to be just and rational, with a good chance of working. Challengers are excellent strategists.

"Explorers go for the creative solution that satisfies their soul. They may bet a long shot, but wow! What an idea!

"Maintainers zero in on the realistic solution that carries the least risk. Rather than being a solution, it might just put things on hold. No gain, but no loss.

"Understand Kingdomality and you can engineer the result *you* want."

"I can see why Peter is successful," said the King. "It's powerful to know what makes people tick. Peter can forecast a person's reaction. He knows what really drives them."

"And Peter can put together balanced teams that are spectacularly productive. No going to war and forgetting supplies," said Lady Elizabeth.

"We know who we are," said Alfred. "That saves

confusion and makes us more productive. We know our gifts and limitations, and we've learned our limitations are the very things others do well."

The King sat down on a nearby rock. "I'm convinced. Teach me more."

"Glad to," said Lady Elizabeth. "I'm going to take you to the Kingdomality Kingdom."

"What's this Kingdomality Kingdom?" asked the King.

"It's a special magical place," said Lady Elizabeth. "Here, in Peter's Kingdom, everyone knows their role, regardless of what their actual job might be. The role names tell you their personality type, not what they do. In the Kingdomality Kingdom, however, people actually live the roles. Role names define not only personality types but also what they actually do. It's the perfect place to learn and understand what Kingdomality really is, and how it works."

CHAPTER FIVE

A VISIT TO THE HELPERS' GUILDHALL

ONCE AGAIN THE KING was to travel via wizard express. This time, though, he was ready.

"We'll be off on a wizard convection current?" asked the King.

"Best way to go," agreed Lady Elizabeth. "No need for Royal Robes. I'll provide something more comfortable."

"That's great," said the King. "These are heavy." He plucked the cloth, but rather than velvet, he grabbed plain material. New clothes! Lady Elizabeth smiled and the King looked around. It was market day, and they were in the midst of a bustling town square within the huge stone walls of what was obviously a very large castle.

"Welcome to the Kingdomality Kingdom," said Lady Elizabeth. "As I told you, this is a magical place, but you can take what you learn here back to your real-life Kingdom and create magic of your own. You've got good people. They just need some Kingdomality magic!"

"Sounds good to me," said the King. "What now?"

"Now we hit the guildhalls. We'll start with that one over there." They crossed the town square to a large stone building where Lady Elizabeth yanked a white silken cord. Beside the door was a bronze plaque:

HELPERS' HALL

Guildhall of White Knights, Dreamer-Minstrels,
and Shepherds Driven to Help, Support,
Nurture, and Make Connections

MOTIVATED BY EMOTIONS

WELCOME

Helpers care about people and how they get along. They are very aware of the people around them and their feelings. Helpers are harmonizers. They dislike discord and feel compelled to make sure that everyone is happy. Helpers are the glue that holds a team together. They serve as cheerleaders for the organization (work, home, church, and so forth) and they provide a sense of humanity and belonging to the group.

Helpers take stands based on their feelings. Feelings, theirs and others, are true facts to Helpers, and they can be puzzled that others can dismiss feelings as not being objective facts. Sometimes being guided by emotions can lead Helpers to make choices that may not turn out to be the best choices, even though the choice feels like the right one at the time. Helpers love to support people, especially if it pleases those being supported. Commitment and connection to a group or cause give life purpose. Helpers can become very passionate about righting what they perceive as a wrong, ofttimes going to lengths and costs other think excessive but which to Helpers are perfectly reasonable.

Helpers will listen intently when the Challengers grouse about the constricting influence of the Maintainers. They encourage Explorers when they are frustrated by the mundane and routine tasks they must perform. They commiserate with Maintainers, who want more structure in the group.

"Welcome, nice to see you again, Lady Elizabeth," said the man who opened the door. He was wearing a long robe and in his hand he carried a shepherd's crook. At his feet on the left was a large sheepdog, and on his right, three of the fluffiest, whitest sheep the King had ever seen.

"I'll bet you're the Shepherd," said the King.

"That's me. And this is my loyal dog Woof and three of my sheep. The rest are out in the yard, if you'd like to meet them?"

"Not right now," said Lady Elizabeth quickly. "Are the White Knight and the Dreamer Minstrel in? I've got a fellow here I'm introducing to the Kingdom. I'll need all of you."

Fellow? Fellow! The King winced slightly and took a deep breath.

"You're in luck," said the Shepherd. "The White Knight is just back from a two-month, fire-breathing dragon hunt."

"Did it pay well?" asked Lady Elizabeth.

"Should. But it didn't. He expected full scale and there was talk of a big bonus, but the appropriation for dragon control has been cut back. Apparently some of the paperwork wasn't right and so he didn't do too well this time. Or last, for that matter," he said sadly. "But he's got some dandy burn marks and lots of great stories. Do come in."

"And the Dreamer-Minstrel?" asked Lady Elizabeth as they passed through the front door.

"Who knows," said the Shepherd, shooing the dog and sheep back inside. "He got up this morning and went off to organize some brass bands. I heard them tromping around the market a little while ago. Our Dreamer-Minstrel likes to end his parades with a speech from the castle balcony telling everyone how wonderful they are. If they give him a standing ovation he won't be home for hours, but lately all he's been getting is a smattering of polite applause, in which case he'll be home any minute."

The door flew open and in marched a tall, middle-aged man dressed in a beautiful suit with white ruffles around the wrists and neck. In his right hand was a brass walking stick. Pure black hair framed a friendly face. He exuded confidence and charisma.

"*I'm home*," he bellowed, as if three others weren't just steps away.

"Our Dreamer-Minstrel," said the Shepherd. "How'd your parade go? And your speech?"

"Parade great. Speech a disaster."

"Well, that speech was a big success the first ten times you gave it," the Shepherd said kindly. "You probably need some new material. I'll help you after dinner. Now I want you to meet somebody. You remember Lady Elizabeth from her last visit. And this is . . . ?"

"Harold. Harold King," said Lady Elizabeth quickly.

"Good to meet you. Especially if you turn out to be a Dreamer-Minstrel. I could use some help," he said as he shook the King's hand. "You're most welcome at Helpers' Hall."

"Take them into the library," said the Shepherd. "I'll let the White Knight know they're here."

The Dreamer-Minstrel led them down the hall and

into a large book-lined room with comfortable chairs and couches.

"Have a seat and let me tell you about Dreamer-Minstreling. Best job in the world."

Before he could say anything more, the door flew open and in strode a cross between the Tin Man from the Wizard of Oz and a knight from King Arthur's Round Table. He was dressed in a suit of armor covered with stickers! "Save the Forest," proclaimed one. "Support Your Favorite Martyr," said another. "Alchemists of the World Unite" was plastered across the visor of his helmet. The overall effect was of a suitcase covered with "I visited . . ." labels. Under the visor was a friendly face that looked wise and yet had the quizzical grin of a ten-year-old catching butterflies.

"Hello there, Lady Elizabeth, Dreamer-Minstrel,"

the armored man said. "And this must be Harold. Good to meet you. I'm the White Knight."

"So what does a White Knight do?" asked the King, or Harold King as he was now, apparently, to be called.

"Do? Why, we do the most important work in the Kingdom. That's what we do. We're the heroes of the Kingdom. You name the cause and we'll fight for it. Provided, of course, it's a good cause. We only do good causes. No right fight is too hopeless for us to take up. Like Don Quixote, we dream the impossible dream and fight the unbeatable foe. My kinda guy. One of the best."

"Some aren't the best?" asked the King.

"Well, to be honest, White Knights sometimes have a few problems."

"Like getting so wrapped up in a fire-eating dragon hunt they forget to be sure they're going to get paid," said the Dreamer-Minstrel, laughing warmly.

"Pay or no pay, someone had to douse its flame before it burned down a forest," said the White Knight defensively.

"But, aside from that, you White Knights are quite perfect then?" asked the King.

"Well, we do tend to wear out and can get a bit theatrical, I suppose."

"A bit theatrical!" exclaimed the Dreamer-Minstrel. "When the White Knight burns out, the whole Kingdom hears his cry of woe and agony. Having experienced the exhilaration of victory, when White Knights experience defeat, sometimes they just can't handle the depths of despair. They whither away with a hurt look that's occasionally replaced with one of stoic satisfaction as they contemplate how heroic they are."

"I admit we can develop a bit of a martyr complex," said the White Knight. "I mean, we suffer so much and endure so much, protecting others from fire-breathing dragons, it *does* become a bit much. Everybody wants a Knight when a dragon is playing barbecue-the-passing-peasant, but as soon as its flame is out, does anybody remember who you are? Not likely! And *then* they stiff us for two months' pay! The Black Knight got his, plus a bonus, for exactly the same work, but they claim that was all by 'prior arrangement.' Well, nobody offered to 'prior arrange' anything with me. All they wanted to arrange was 'How fast can you get here?' I mean, wouldn't you feel put upon?" the White Knight demanded in a rapidly rising voice.

The White Knight's tirade, it turned out, was just getting started.

"It's all very well for the rest of you. Stay home while I'm out getting my fingers burned to a crisp putting the fire extinguisher into the dragon's mouth. And what do I ask for? Well, pay *would* be nice. Very nice indeed, but a simple thank-you would be nice too." The White Knight continued with evident anger and hurt, "This isn't the first time, you know." He began listing a number of incidents that had brought forth neither reward nor praise. Of the two, the White Knight was obviously far more concerned about lack of praise.

In mid-complaint the White Knight stomped off out of the room. The door slammed closed behind him as he continued to rant about the hard life he led and the little or no thanks he got for everything he did for everyone else.

"He's sure helped a lot of ungrateful people," said the King.

"Not necessarily," said the Dreamer-Minstrel. "Helpers have a high need for feedback and praise. White Knights in particular. Praise that would satisfy an Explorer or Maintainer, and seem excessive to a Challenger, can leave a White Knight feeling unappreciated.

"Don't forget, you've caught our White Knight when he's stressed and most prone to be, as he said, a 'bit theatrical.' When he's on the job, though, the job gets done, even if that means he sometimes has to use his weapons. That sword of his is sharp, and while he hesitates to draw it unless absolutely necessary, he is a knight and can fight. White Knights really do make the world a better place."

Before more could be said, the door opened again. The Shepherd entered, this time without either the dog or the sheep. "Sorry I was delayed. I wanted to get the sheep settled. Wasn't that the White Knight storming out? What happened?"

"Nothing, nothing at all," said the Dreamer-Minstrel. "We had a delightful visit."

"Bosh," said the Shepherd. "He's going on about pay and thanks, isn't he?"

"Well . . ." said the Dreamer-Minstrel.

"Don't worry. He'll find a new cause by the end of the week and be flying high again," said the Shepherd, who then turned to Harold, our King, and said, "and you've learned something about Dreamer-Minstrels, too. They're the public relations people of the Kingdom. The spin doctors. Our White Knight goes off the deep end and the Dreamer-Minstrel wants to gloss it over. Calls it a 'delightful visit.' Our Dreamer-Minstrel can find the silver lining in any situation and the pot of gold at the end of every rainbow."

"It *was* a delightful visit, at least right until nearly the end," objected the Dreamer-Minstrel.

"I'm sure it was," said the Shepherd, "for all of three minutes. You *do* tend to be the optimist of the Kingdom and take a bit of poetic license with the facts, you know," he added with such fondness that the King almost expected him to reach out and give a fatherly rumple to the Dreamer-Minstrel's hair.

"You're very kind to say so," said the Dreamer-Minstrel. "As for the White Knight, I'm sure it will all work out for the best. Everything does, you know. Now, I must ask you to excuse me. I'm sorry that I have to leave, but I did promise to help cook if I got home early enough."

The King and Lady Elizabeth said good-bye and promised to try to make his next speech. The Shepherd walked over to the door with him, and the King quietly asked Lady Elizabeth, "Am I right? Did I hear the Dreamer-Minstrel *thank* the Shepherd for saying he took 'poetic license with the facts'?"

"You did."

"I think I'd be miffed, not pleased," whispered the King.

"That's because you're not a Dreamer-Minstrel. It's not lying, or even white lies, to him. He'd call it creatively ignoring some things to highlight only the best. Others might think it not objective. The Dreamer-

Minstrel sees it as a talent to separate the important from the irrelevant."

"Isn't he wonderful? We're very proud of our Dreamer-Minstrel, and our White Knight too, for that matter," said the Shepherd, turning from the door.

Their good-byes to the Shepherd at the guildhall front door were interrupted by the White Knight's voice bellowing from a window above.

"He can't do that! Wait till I get there."

The White Knight came roaring down the staircase. *"Outta the way. Coming through."*

"Just a minute," said the Shepherd, planting himself in front of the door.

"Outta my way, Shepherd. No time. No time."

"Not until you tell me where you're going and when you're coming back. Really coming back," said the Shepherd firmly.

"I'm not leaving the castle," said the White Knight. "Hagor the Hunter has been poaching unicorns again. I'm going to his house to straighten this out once and for all. If they keep hunting unicorns out of season, they'll soon be extinct!"

"Be home for supper, mind you," said the Shepherd as he stepped aside and the White Knight went flying past.

"As predicted," he said to the King and Lady Elizabeth. "All his troubles, not getting paid or thanked for his dragon work, are forgotten. And what a cause! Extinct! The woods are full of unicorns. White Knights sure can get worked up over nothing."

"They certainly can," said Lady Elizabeth. "We must be off. I'll be in touch."

A mixed bag these Helpers, the King decided as they followed the White Knight out the door, but they did have several things in common:

- They did like to help! At least what they saw as being helpful. Others, thought the King, just might think Helpers were poking their noses into others' business.

- Shepherds, White Knights, Dreamer-Minstrels, not one of them liked any sort of conflict. If one word could sum them up, it might be harmony. As go-along, get-along, harmonious people they all were likeable, showed appreciation of others easily, and, in return, liked lots of recognition for what they did for others.

· Not only did they make decisions based on emotions (gut feelings), they also reacted to others emotionally. They could be moody, hurt, happy, or upset, depending on what others said or did. Helpers, concluded the King, take the world personally and expect the world to take them seriously and treat them fairly.

DOWN SOUTH, AND AT THE BOTTOM
OF THE SUNDIAL, ARE THE EMOTIONAL HELPERS.

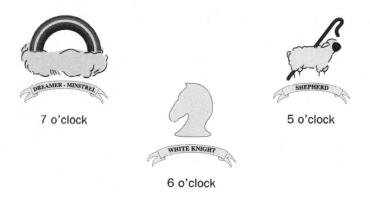

7 o'clock   5 o'clock

6 o'clock

CHAPTER SIX

A VISIT TO THE CHALLENGERS' GUILDHALL

*T*HE NEXT STOP, said Lady Elizabeth, would be the Challengers' Guildhall. "As you know, Challengers are as different from Helpers as you can get. We'll go there next."

"Sounds good to me," said the King. "Tell me, what's with this name, Harold King?"

"Sorry. Let me explain. Ordinary people, and remember you're meeting ordinary Kingdomality subjects, can become quite tongue-tied around royalty. It works better if you're just Harold."

"I've never been plain people before. It's interesting.

And you're right. People certainly treat you differently. They're more open. Natural, I guess. I confess I like it."

"Thought you might," said Lady Elizabeth. "It's tough for a king to really understand ordinary people. Kings always think they are in touch and know what it's like for the people they rule. That delusion shows how out of touch they are!"

This same delusion remains rampant today among corporate Royalty, who can be found masquerading as "The Boss" at all levels of an organization. In a flash of magic, equal to the best of even the most worthy wizard, many ordinary people, upon being named "The Boss," are transformed instantly into corporate Royalty, soon losing touch with former friends and coworkers. Worse, almost, is that they think they're still in touch!

"Another thing I want you to keep in mind," said Lady Elizabeth, "is that here in the Kingdomality Kingdom, most of the people we'll meet actually live the roles. Out in the real world, most White Knights aren't knights at all."

"Got it," said the King. "But it does help me remember when I meet them in their Kingdomality roles."

"It does. First, though, understand the four main groups. The essential thing to know about Helpers is that they're driven by emotion, how they feel. Challengers, whom we meet next, are the opposite. They're driven by logical thinking."

"Okay, answer me this, then. What's the difference between the White Knight, the Dreamer-Minstrel, and the Shepherd? I can see they're different. But why's that?"

"Good question," said Lady Elizabeth as they approached the Challenger's Guildhall.

"You'll recall on our sundial that the White Knight is at the bottom, at six o'clock. Shepherds are on the right, at five o'clock—nearer to Maintainer territory, over in what would be the east on a map."

"I remember Maintainers are the realists. They're centered around three o'clock on our sundial," said the King.

"Good for you," said Lady Elizabeth, and picking up a long stick, she drew a circle in the sandy ground. "White Knights at six, Shepherds at five, and the Dreamer-Minstrel at seven o'clock."

"And the Scientist is at three and the Bishop at nine o'clock," said the King.

"Representing which main groups?"

"The Scientist is a Maintainer on the east side. The Bishop, an Explorer on the west."

"Right. Here's what it looks like so far," said Lady Elizabeth.

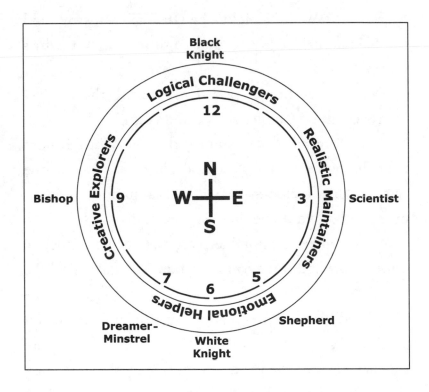

"As you can see, Shepherds are closer to Maintainer territory than the Dreamer-Minstrels who are on the Explorer side. The reason is that Shepherds have some Maintainer in their makeup, and Dreamer-Minstrels have some Explorer."

The King looked at the sundial and noted the distinguishing characteristic of each group. "So, Shepherds would be emotionally realistic, whereas Dreamer-Minstrels are emotionally creative."

"That's right," said Lady Elizabeth. "Shepherds have a secondary preference, which is the Maintainer's realistic approach to life, and the Dreamer-Minstrel's secondary preference is the creativity of Explorers.

"Another thing you need to be aware of," she said, "is that every White Knight isn't exactly like every other White Knight. Think of the sundial as a circle, a wheel. That circle has a center, a hub, and it has an edge, the rim. If a spoke on the wheel were to run from where I've marked the White Knight on the rim, to the hub in the center, all along that spoke would be White Knights. But the ones at the edge, on the rim, would have far more intense, or pronounced, White Knight characteristics than those closer to the hub in the center. Here in the Kingdomality Kingdom the people you are meeting are all out on the edge. You'll rarely see that sort of intensity outside this magical kingdom."

The King asked, "If my subjects are not so near the edge, closer to the center, that's going to make it harder to recognize their Kingdomality role, isn't it?"

"It will," said Lady Elizabeth, "but don't forget, close to the center or out on the edge, a White Knight is a White Knight is a White Knight. Some just aren't so in-your-face about it."

With that they continued across the square. Challengers' Hall looked remarkably like Helpers' Hall, right down to the plaque outside the door.

CHALLENGERS' HALL

Guildhall of Merchants, Black Knights, and Prime Ministers
Driven to Win and Be Efficient

MOTIVATED BY LOGICAL THINKING

ENTRANCE BY ADMISSION ONLY

Challengers are strategists who pursue the most efficient and logical path toward the realization of their plans. Logical thinking is their strength. Challengers are the competitors of the world. They constantly challenge themselves and the people around them. Challengers have a great need to know what the score is, and they will rarely play a game for the fun of it. Challengers are motivated to make constant improvements; that is how they define growth, even life itself. Better, faster, cheaper is more than a slogan for them; it is a way of life.

Challengers are results oriented. Their competitive impulses may cause them to emphasize competition over teamwork. This can result in short-term success, but sometimes the cost of short-term success can be long-term discord and infighting.

Challengers don't easily accept goals others set for them. They typically have little regard for policies and procedures. If an organization's policies stand in the way of a Challenger, the policies will be circumvented or ignored. Challengers can keep prodigious amounts of data that will help support their goal. Challengers make excellent entrepreneurs.

Challengers focus Explorers, spur Maintainers to action, and keep Helpers from becoming so emotional that they become ineffective.

"What's this 'Entrance by Admission Only'?" asked the King.

"Typical Challenger talk," said Lady Elizabeth. "Challengers like to get paid. Black Knights are Challengers. Remember the Black Knight got paid for the dragon hunt when the White Knight didn't? See where it says that logical thinking is what motivates Challengers?"

"I do."

"Well, what could be more logical than making sure you get paid? Challengers think that if we take up their time, then we should pay an admission charge."

"And you pay?"

"We objected, of course, but in the end the Master of Kingdomality Roles negotiated a blanket yearly fee. It used to be difficult to see Challengers because they were

so busy. Now they're glad to see us."

"Lady Elizabeth! Welcome to Challenger's Hall," came a voice from within.

As the King's eyes adjusted to the light, he had no doubt it was the Merchant greeting them. The Merchant wore a smock and a green eye-shade, and the half-moon spectacles perched on his nose gave him a quizzical look that reminded the King of Mr. Saffie of Saffie's Royal Robes who had outfitted him when he was a young prince.

"Hello, Merchant. May we come in?" asked Lady Elizabeth.

"Your yearly pass guarantees your welcome."

"This is Harold King," said Lady Elizabeth. "Harold, meet the Merchant."

"Pleased," said the King.

"Likewise," said the Merchant. "The Prime Minister is here, but you've just missed the Black Knight. Apparently Hagor has been after the Unicorns again and the Black Knight has been called in to straighten things out. I'll send for him."

"Unicorn poaching!" said Lady Elizabeth with mock alarm. "I bet the Black Knight will get a good fee for that."

"He has a satisfactory arrangement," said the Merchant. "I gave him a hand with the contract. I do all his contracts."

"Sounds like he's lucky to have you," said the King.

"I like to think so," replied the Merchant. "I love doing a deal. A well-structured deal is a thing of beauty. I do lots of my own deals, but the Black Knight has interesting ones to work on. I keep track of the details and figure out the angles for him."

"Angles?" questioned Lady Elizabeth.

"Lots of angles. Ten percent of the booty is worth squat unless you've covered all the angles. Is that before or after commission? Who values the booty? Does the cut for Royalty come off the top, or is the booty inclusive? Regardless of percentage, who gets first pick? Then there's override for subsequent conquest facilitated by current conquest. Each needs to be considered. Only last year I convinced the Black Knight to give up two percentage points of immediate booty in return for a two-percent override on subsequent booty, and to date he's nearly doubled his take."

"Nice deal," said the King.

"They're all nice deals," said the Merchant, "provided you take the time to analyze every contingency and plan for it. Now if you'll excuse me, I'll go get the Prime Minister. Please make yourselves comfortable."

The King said, "Let me guess. If the Black Knight is at twelve o'clock on the sundial, and that's the home of logical thinking, then the Merchant has to be over on the Maintainer side, the realistic thinkers, right? At one o'clock."

"That's the Merchant. Logically realistic. And Prime Ministers are logically creative, which puts them at eleven o'clock. I think you'll be interested in the engraving on the tabletop over there," said Lady Elizabeth.

The King walked over and looking down saw a much-abbreviated sundial etched into the tabletop.

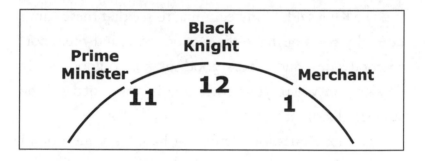

"These Challengers don't waste engraving, do they?" said the King.

"No they don't," agreed Lady Elizabeth. "Challengers can be efficient and focused, and logically realistic Merchants are notoriously careful. They don't like to waste anything, especially an opportunity, and so they like to keep their options open just in case a deal might be improved. The concept of perfect isn't too perfect to a Merchant. As long as a deal is open, they can continue to assess their position and monitor the changing risks and rewards. If you want to see a look of pure horror on a Merchant's face, suggest you flip a coin to decide an important issue in a deal, especially if you're trying to save time. Merchants like time to think and rethink and don't like to be pushed before they're ready."

The King said, "I'm beginning to see that these Kingdomality roles all have their good sides and their not-so-good sides, and what's good, or not so good, really depends on where your own role is positioned on the sundial, doesn't it?"

"It's not a question of good or bad. It's a question of preferences," said Lady Elizabeth. "Your role position on the sundial is a result of your preferences."

Lady Elizabeth was cut off by the door opening and in came the Merchant, followed by a woman who could only be described as handsome. Not beautiful, not cute, not plain, not striking. Handsome.

She was, perhaps, forty. She would have looked serene and peaceful were it not for her gray eyes, which flicked from face to face and then around the room, missing nothing. Handsome certainly, but the other word that leapt to the King's mind was shrewd. She had the look of someone who knew more than she'd ever say.

"I've found her. Down in the basement, in a meeting," said the Merchant.

"Kind of you to come up, Prime Minister," said Lady Elizabeth. "We won't keep you long."

"No you won't," said the Prime Minister, not rudely, not forcefully, and without the slightest trace of hostility. She was simply stating a fact, she wouldn't be with them long. The King, who wasn't used to being spoken to so abruptly, felt partly annoyed and yet partly abashed for having interrupted her business.

"Good to see you again, Prime Minister," Lady Elizabeth said to her, and then to the King she said, "Prime Ministers can be very direct and even blunt. Don't read anything more into what she says than what she says. Prime Ministers say what they mean and mean what they say."

"You're right, I didn't mean to be abrupt, if that's what I was. And welcome to Challengers' Hall, Harold King," said the Prime Minister. The King felt she knew exactly who he was. Her next words as much as confirmed this. "I've heard of your arrival in *our* Kingdom."

"Thanks. Sorry to bother you. Important meeting, no doubt?" asked the King.

"Oh, just some people."

"Ha!" said the Merchant. "I recognized four of the six people and each was what the town crier calls an 'important personage.' They didn't look happy. I suspect the Prime Minister was laying down the law again."

"Merchant, you should have been an Explorer, the way your imagination is running away with you," said the Prime Minister.

"Tell it to Corrit the Crusader," muttered the Merchant.

"Enough," said the Prime Minister firmly. "Now, I must get back to my meeting, but I did want to say hello to Harold King."

"Who is Corrit the Crusader?" asked the King when she was gone.

"Former confidant to the Prime Minister," said the Merchant. "I say former because the Prime Minister trusted Corrit with an important job that wasn't completed to the Prime Minister's satisfaction, despite her spending time with Corrit to explain her expectations. Since then, Corrit is history around here, and perhaps even the Kingdom."

"Sounds ruthless," said the King.

"Perhaps, but the Prime Minister sees it as creative problem solving aimed at an efficient result. She is always willing to give people a chance. Sometimes two. And the Prime Minister is always thinking of more productive ways to achieve the result she wants. But if an idea or a person doesn't work out, she will make a move. No doubt about it: She doesn't suffer fools gladly."

"Why would she be meeting in the basement?" asked the King. "That's a strange place to hold what sounds like an important meeting."

"It's not strange to a Prime Minister," replied Lady Elizabeth. "Prime Ministers like to work behind the scenes, rolling up their sleeves, analyzing the problem, pulling strings, rewarding, challenging, doing whatever it takes to reach their goal. They are the power brokers of the kingdom and very focused on results. They're far less concerned about getting credit than they are about getting a quality job done."

"She certainly was efficient in the time she was with us. A quick 'hello,' then she was gone," said the King.

The Merchant replied, "Prime Ministers are very focused on the strategy for getting what they want. The fact is, there wasn't anything she wanted from us right then, and she had things to do at her meeting. What could be more logical than to cut us short? And don't forget, Prime Ministers are creative. She'd want to meet Harold, see if she might use him in any way. I assure you, all the way going back down the stairs she's thinking about what she's learned here, and she's also setting her strategy for when she reenters her meeting. Prime Ministers are exceptional strategists."

"They can also seem unforgiving and controlling to some other types," added Lady Elizabeth. "Some would see this as a negative, but a Prime Minister doesn't. They can be forgiving, and patient, and understanding, but only up to a reasonable point. Beyond that, they'd say it was time to take action, insist on performance, or make a change. That's the logical thing to do. Prime Ministers will tell you that insanity is doing more of the same thing and expecting different results. When being forgiving, patient, and understanding doesn't produce results, they think it's insane to keep doing the same thing. As for 'controlling,' Prime Ministers see that as a compliment. That's what life is all about. A river without banks is just a large puddle, and puddles don't go anywhere or accomplish anything."

A clanging sound from the doorway caused the King, Lady Elizabeth, and the Merchant to swing their heads around in time to see the Black Knight stride in, dressed in full armor.

BLACK KNIGHT

"Only a fool suffers a fool," said the Black Knight as he entered and began to strip off his armor, which matched that of the White Knight, except there were no "Save the World" stickers on his well-oiled helmet or chest plate.

"Finished with Hagor quickly, did you?" said the Merchant.

"Finished Hagor was more like it," replied the Black Knight.

"I discovered the White Knight trying to talk him out of Unicorn poaching because it was bad for the ecology. Imagine! Hagor's about to have roast Unicorn and a cold beer and the White Knight thinks he'll give a fig for the environment! I stormed in and reminded Hagor that last time I promised I'd make an example of him. The White Knight started to tell me Hagor's problem goes back to being abandoned by his mother for a sailor from a ship called *Unicorn*. While he was talking I whipped out my sword, whacked off Hagor's right ear, and told him next time I'd clip off a hand."

"I bet that upset the White Knight," said Lady Elizabeth.

"More than it did Hagor," said the Black Knight, "and it was Hagor's ear. Strange man, that White Knight. Just kept going at me about Hagor's supposed mother trouble, and his impoverished childhood, until I told him my mother had run off with a sailor from the good ship *White Knight* and if he didn't shut up I'd let my inner child out and do a little poaching myself."

"Another great success," said the Merchant. "We got half the money up front. I'll send out your invoice for the balance immediately."

"Sure beats the land reform deal, doesn't it?" the Black Knight said to the Merchant.

"Land reform deal?" questioned the King.

The Merchant said, "It was a problem with some peasants squatting on private land. We took no money up front, but we had a nice participation on the land. Unfortunately, there were a lot more peasants and they were a lot better armed than the Black Knight expected. Facing a long and costly campaign, he turned around and headed home to cut his losses. It was the smart and logical thing to do. Thanks to a reverse nonperformance clause I'd inserted into the contract, he was on solid ground."

"Solid ground or no solid ground, I don't fight dumb fights," said the Black Knight. "Now, I'd best go have a bath. Please excuse me."

"Good cue for us to be on our way," said Lady Elizabeth. "I think Harold's got a good idea of what Challengers are like."

Back outside once again the King said, "Challengers seem to share three things:

· They challenge others and they challenge themselves—bigger, better, faster, more accurate, more comprehensive, more, more, more of everything!

· If it isn't logical—if it doesn't make sense—they don't do it.

· They're all very focused on results, setting a goal and achieving it. They take personal responsibility for results and hold others responsible too."

Lady Elizabeth smiled. "That's the Challengers. We're ready to visit our next main Kingdomality group. Let's visit the Maintainers. No Kingdom can run long or well without Maintainers."

Lady Elizabeth was right about Maintainers. However, the same applies equally to Challengers, Helpers, and Explorers. At any one point one personality type might be of more immediate importance than another, but over time all are of equal value. An enduring, lasting organization needs all four to be successful: Creative Explorers to find new products, approaches, and profit centers; Realistic Maintainers to ensure stability and compliance by collecting receivables, paying payables, and being sure occupancy permits and tax returns are current; Logical Challengers to push forward and demand efficiencies and effective approaches to solving problems; and

Emotional Helpers to unify, coordinate, facilitate, and create conditions that allow everyone to contribute their best.

UP NORTH, AT THE TOP OF THE SUNDIAL,

ARE THE LOGICAL CHALLENGERS.

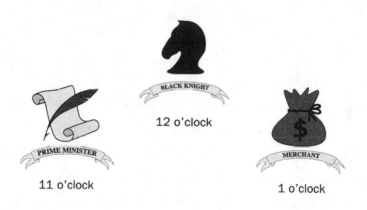

12 o'clock

11 o'clock

1 o'clock

CHAPTER SEVEN

A VISIT TO THE MAINTAINERS' GUILDHALL

ON THE EAST SIDE of the square sat the Maintainers' Guildhall and beside the door was a plaque. A garden of flowers to the right of the door was perfectly groomed. No dead or even faded blossoms. Half were white, half red. It could have been a pleasing mixture, but the left side was red and the right white!

"That's a bit strange, isn't it?" asked the King.

"Not as strange as how it got that way," replied Lady Elizabeth. "The garden used to be all red. Very nice, but a little boring. Some visiting Explorers suggested it might look a little better with a mixture of colors. Maintainers wouldn't hear of it. Red was good enough for their fathers and good enough for their grandfathers, and red was good enough for them. Finally the Explorers got the Maintainers to agree to try adding white. But when the Explorers saw what the Maintainers did the next year, they gave up. There are exactly 327 red on the right and 327 white on the left.

"Maintainers plant on May twenty-fourth and the garden is ripped out and the soil turned on September eighteenth, regardless of the weather. It gets watered on Tuesday afternoon for two hours, rain or shine. The Maintainers are actually quite proud of their flowers. They call it the Explorers' garden."

"When did these Explorers visit?" wondered the King, thinking perhaps in a year or two the garden might change.

"Two hundred years ago," said Lady Elizabeth. "Just yesterday to a Maintainer."

"I think I'm beginning to get a feel for these Maintainers already. Let's have a look at their plaque," said the King.

MAINTAINERS' HALL

Guildhall of Engineer-Builders, Scientists, and Doctors
We Seek to Make Things Work Continually
Day After Day After Day

MOTIVATED BY REALISTIC THINKING

Maintainers have a strong sense of right and wrong and see situations as black and white. They are exceptionally organized and detail oriented. Maintainers have a conservative outlook and high regard for the chain of command. Rules and authority are important concepts for Maintainers. They derive a sense of place and constancy from the steady and reliable influence of rules and laws. No detail is too small for their scrutiny, no force too powerful that can't be harnessed by the assiduous application of the rule. Maintainers have no fondness for chaos. They feel compelled to bring order to disorder. "A place for everything, and everything in its place" is the motto of the Maintainer. They communicate their plans in simple, straightforward statements. Maintainers can have trouble seeing the necessity for change that others do, and may be seen as unreasonable and rigid by others.

Maintainers provide a sense of consistency, prudence, and order for an organization. Their talents contribute to the success of an organization by tempering the Explorer's lust for chaos, defining and depersonalizing the Helper's decisions, and buffering the Challenger's aversion to rules and details.

"The flower bed tells the story, doesn't it?" mused the King as he read the plaque. "I bet, just from the names, I can tell where they fit on the sundial. I already know the Scientist is at three o'clock. Engineer-Builders have to have a goal-setting, perfection-driving Challenger strain, so I'd put them at two o'clock, making them realistically logical. The Doctors have to be part Helper, so they'd be at four o'clock and would be realistically emotional. Not a bad thing for a doctor, when you think about it."

"Good for you," said Lady Elizabeth.

The King crouched down and started to mark out a sundial on the ground.

"Good again. Let's see who is at home. Although Maintainers aren't much for going out to someplace new without a compelling reason for doing so," said Lady Elizabeth, hand raised to knock, when the door swung open and an ancient lady came tottering out.

"Take two at bedtime and come back in three days," said a voice. A moment later the doctor appeared. Long red hair hung to her shoulders and freckles splashed across her nose and cheeks. Her smile was warm, wide, and wonderful.

When she spotted Lady Elizabeth, her smile lit up her whole face. "Why Lady Elizabeth, it's been ages!"

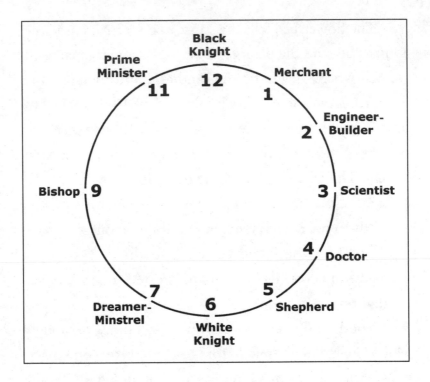

In quick order the Doctor ushered Lady Elizabeth and the King into the guildhall's central parlor.

"Your timing is perfect," she said. "My office hours are finished, the Engineer-Builder is home from the job site—a new dam over the east river—and it's time we dragged our Scientist out of the dungeon."

"The dungeon?" asked the King.

"That's what I call it. He calls it a lab. Safe and secret down under the guildhall, he blends his powders and liquids searching for knowledge. Truth. The eternal. Useful is nice, but a Scientist is thrilled if the knowledge he discovers is pure. Scientific method is the essence of Kingdomality Scientists. Rules and regulations, policies and procedures, tried and true, right way, wrong way, order, order, order.

"Scientists are the straight arrows of Kingdomality and proud of it. Their major joy in life is to be allowed to develop, analyze, and critique new ideas. Explorers like a new idea every minute. Scientists can be happy working on one idea for a lifetime.[1]"

"I can see how Scientist fits with Maintainer," said the King, "but Doctor? That sounds more Explorer to me, although I confess I haven't been to their guildhall

---

[1] A visitor is said to have commiserated with Edison's failure after the great inventor had tried 1,132 lightbulb elements and none worked. Edison was horrified. It wasn't a failure! He now knew 1,132 elements that didn't work, he replied.

yet—but aren't those the creative people? And Doctors make sick people well, so isn't that Explorer?"

"Oh, no! No, no, no," said the Doctor. "Doctors put people back the way they're supposed to be and also strive to prevent problems. We don't improve on healthy people. In reality, we're often doing well to keep people from getting worse, maintaining them at whatever level they're at. Remember our credo: First, do no harm. Above all, our mission is to maintain the status quo."

"Sometimes," said Lady Elizabeth, "Doctors can put tradition ahead of innovation, even when the innovation may be helpful to patients."

"Really?" said the King. The Doctor looked uncomfortable.

"Yes, really," replied Lady Elizabeth. "Doctors are very slow to start using new medicines or techniques. Especially if they are revolutionary. They prefer a gradual shift. They may tirelessly seek new knowledge and ways of perfecting the procedures they follow, but they prefer orderly progression, just as Scientists do. Each step building on the last, and each tested by repetition. All being revealed in the fullness of time is far more satisfactory than explosive enlightenment."

"Why's that? I'd have thought fast would be valued. At least it would to me, if I were sick," said the King.

"We don't see it as a shortcoming," said the Doctor. "We might lose a patient, but that's a single patient. If we were to plunge ahead with every new unproven fad or idea, many might die. The result could be chaos. Doctors have a need for order and we like structure. Doctors like to practice in groups, to form associations, to establish hospitals. All with their own rules and regulations, policies and procedures with the single aim of maintaining consistent comfort and treatment. Not only for patients, not only for society, but also for ourselves. In the end our overriding goal is to maintain the status quo."

"I can see that now," said the King. "Both the Scientist and the Doctor fit perfectly into the Maintainer group. As for the Engineer-Builder . . ."

"As for the Engineer-Builder," came a voice from above, "he is the perfect Maintainer. We're realistically logical."

Looking up, the King saw an elderly gentleman walking along the balcony that circled the top of the room. At the top of the staircase he began to descend. In one hand the Engineer-Builder carried a book. On his head was a strange-looking metal hat.

"Thanks for coming down," said Lady Elizabeth. "Is that a new book?"

"Had it since my university days," said the Engineer-Builder with pride. "In one volume I've got the building code, unabridged mind you, unabridged, and the temperature coefficients for the expansion of both copper and lead. *Thomson's Concordance of Estimating* and *Wiswell on Design* are included, as are all safety rules and regulations."

"And the hat?" asked Lady Elizabeth.

"It's called a hard hat. I'm thinking of doing up a rule that says they have to be worn by everyone on a job site. Headwear is totally unregulated now. On the other hand, no sense fixing something that isn't broken."

"How goes the new dam?" asked Lady Elizabeth.

"Disaster. Absolute disaster," said the Engineer-Builder. "The politicians want it built one way and the Local Area Advisory Group wants it built another. Not one of them has ever built a dam before and yet they all want a say. Why the know-nothings can't keep out of the way of people who know what they're doing and let us get on with the job, I'll never know! Most frustrating job I've ever had."

"That's what you said about the last one. The reorganization of the National Property Registry," the Doctor said.

"Don't mention that!" said the Engineer-Builder in mock horror. "They put the Bishop from the Explorers' group in charge of that job, and even though Kingdomality has taught me every viewpoint has value, that man near drove me nuts. First one thing, then another, and just when you thought you knew what he wanted, he wanted something else. Total chaos. That Bishop couldn't make up his mind if he wanted a window open or closed in a snowstorm."

"I can see how Engineer-Builders are Maintainers," said the King.

"You should meet the Scientist!" said Lady Elizabeth.

A loud bang thundered up a stone staircase on the far side of the room.

"Oh dear," said the Doctor.

"Damn, damn, damn. Damn it all anyways," came echoing up the staircase, followed by a belch of black smoke. A moment later a man in a soot-darkened lab coat came stumbling up the stairs coughing and cussing.

"Is Sniffy all right?" asked the Doctor anxiously.

The Scientist stuck his hand into the side pocket of his lab coat. "Yup, he's fine." A white furry face with

SCIENTIST

a pink nose poked up over the edge of the pocket. The nose twitched twice and then popped back down into the pocket.

"Nap time," said the Doctor by way of explanation for Sniffy's departure.

"I'd have thought that explosion would keep him awake for the rest of the day," said the King.

"Not Sniffy," said the Scientist. "He's used to them."

"Do you have many explosions?" queried the King.

"Couple of times a week, lately. Getting better though," said the Scientist proudly. "Few years ago I was blowing up the lab most every day. Back in my father's time, he'd blow in the morning and most afternoons, but we're learning."

"And what are you learning?" asked the King.

The Scientist began a long explanation of the experiments he and his father had been conducting over the years, which had to do with combining various com-

pounds under different conditions. "The humidity variant in the catalyst chamber is critical if it's going to
remain stable and not blow."

"Perhaps less heat might do the trick," ventured the
King. "If I've understood you right, it tends to blow, as
you put it, when it gets hot."

The Scientist looked aghast at the thought. "The
hypothesis is that the humidity variant is the determinant, not the heat."

"But when you heat it . . . ."

"Humidity variant, that's the issue. Not heat," said
the Scientist.

"All right," said the King, who decided further discussion wasn't going to be productive. "Tell me, then,
what are you making?"

"One thing I'm not making is explosions," said the
Scientist. "At least I won't be when I get it right."

"But aside from right, what do you have? What is
it for?"

The Scientist gave the King a blank stare. "You
don't *do* anything with it. At least I don't think you do.
What you do do is combine the elements under conditions that don't cause an explosion by controlling the
humidity variant. That's what you do."

"Two things you need to understand," said Lady Elizabeth. "Scientists can get so focused that they miss possibilities that don't fit neatly into their plan. After they've exhausted the string of hard evidence, they'll likely backtrack and pick up the scent of truth where they veered off. But in the meantime, they can bark long and hard up the wrong tree. In the same vein, Scientists are not particularly good at pure speculation or hypothesizing because their minds are trained to focus only on what's known, not what's unknown.

"Second, the Scientist's experiments don't necessarily lead to the kinds of things others would call useful. Scientists are glad if people can find a use for the knowledge they unearth, but the quest is for the knowledge, for truth; experimental facts that can be replicated and added to the body of things we know to be true. Useful is nice. True is . . . is ?" said Lady Elizabeth, searching for the right word.

"Truth is beautiful, it's pure, it's sacred," supplied the Scientist. "It's the closest to Holy that mankind can come." Then he said to the King, "You've met us all now. Not extensive enough for a proper report, but tell me, what nuggets of beautiful truth have you uncovered about Maintainers?"

"Let's see," said the King. "Maintainers are the realists of the Kingdom:

- They don't like chaos, don't like change, but they do like order and consistency. Tried and true is more than a value, it's a way of life. Bringing order and clarity is their mission in life.

- Rules and regulations are the guides by which they live and seek order and clarity.

- They don't see shades of gray. Things are right or wrong, black or white. Or, in the case of flower gardens, red and white."

Lady Elizabeth smiled warmly to show her approval and said, "I think we're ready to head for the last guild-hall. Home of the Explorers."

"Explorers!" the three Maintainers cried out in unison.

"Nice people, but crazy as a cut cat," said the Engineer-Builder. "They build roads just to see where they wind up. Ridiculous!"

The Doctor gave an involuntary shudder. "If they're

sick, they do the most bizarre things to themselves without a shred of scientific proof it will work."

"Chaos," grumbled the Scientist. "Total chaos over there. Lots of projects, lots of change, lots of new ideas and new events, but no plan, no policies, no rules, no procedures, at least none that last longer than a week."

IN THE EAST, ON THE RIGHT-HAND SIDE OF THE
SUNDIAL, ARE THE REALISTIC MAINTAINERS.

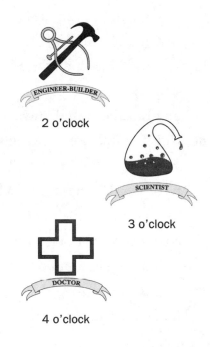

2 o'clock

3 o'clock

4 o'clock

CHAPTER EIGHT

A VISIT TO THE EXPLORERS' GUILDHALL

*T*HE EXTERIOR of the Explorers' Guildhall was unlike the others. The first three halls had been made of stone, with windows and flat walls and square corners. The Explorers' hall didn't have a square corner to it. All swirls and curves. Stones and timbers defined open spaces.

The guildhall had a plaque, but it was suspended in midair, twirling at the end of a golden chain dangling from a timber poking out of the top floor like a flagpole. The King reached up and steadied the plaque so he could read it.

EXPLORERS' HALL

*Guildhall of Benevolent Rulers, Bishops, and
Discoverers Seekers of New Experiences*

LOVERS OF CREATIVITY

Explorers are visionary leaders, fascinated by the future. Explorers are very interested in new things (cutting-edge technology, the latest fashion, the newest trend) and are typically very creative. They are inventors and "possibility thinkers." They can become so wrapped up in the future that what's going on around them in the present isn't noticed. They can seem absentminded, disorganized, and distracted. Explorers are very comfortable with change. They are, in fact, always seeking out new experiences. They thrive in chaotic environments because they know that chaos, rather than necessity, is the true mother of invention.

The Explorers' vision often doesn't reflect true present circumstances but rather future possibilities. Accordingly, Explorers are, by nature, often impractical and unrealistic.

Explorers are typically not very skilled socially. They tend to be unaware of the everyday needs of the people around them. They can become so wrapped up in their own thoughts and visions that they neglect the social niceties that keep groups working smoothly.

Explorers encourage Maintainers to try new things, help Challengers see the rewards of change, and push Helpers to move on and let old, failed relationships and issues die.

"So this is where the King is," said the King with some satisfaction. "Benevolent Ruler. I'm looking forward to meeting him."

"Sorry. Wrong on both counts," replied Lady Elizabeth. "The Benevolent Ruler is not the King here. Remember, I told you that any personality type could be King. Benevolent Ruler is simply a name for a personality style. But I'll grant they can sometimes be a bit bossy! And second, the Benevolent Ruler here is a her, not a him."

"Well, I'd still like to meet this 'her,'" said the King. "Where is she?"

"Good question. Good question for any Explorer. Maintainers don't like to leave home to go anywhere new or unfamiliar. Explorers just love to be out and off."

"No bell cord to yank here," said the King, looking around.

"Not Explorer style," said Lady Elizabeth. "We'll just go on in. The door is always open," she said as she turned and walked in between two stone pillars.

"Helloooo! Helloooo!" called out Lady Elizabeth, but to no apparent avail.

"No one's home," said the King.

"Not necessarily," she said. "Could be they're all

meditating, or simply too interested in whatever it is they're doing to bother responding. Let's look around."

The two set off, poking their heads into various rooms and chambers and finding them all empty. At the back of the Explorers' Guildhall they discovered a large room where someone was swinging in a wicker basket suspended from the cathedral ceiling by a strong chain.

"Excuse me, have you seen the Benevolent Ruler? Or, for that matter, the Bishop or the Discoverer?" asked Lady Elizabeth.

An ancient face, wrinkled by too much sun at an early age, poked up over the edge of the basket and, giving a toothless grin, said, "Beezle boss, bye bethelwait. Dollas dames dimilglat."

"Thank you very much," said Lady Elizabeth and, turning around, set off back toward the front door.

"Perry pokus pilike pollanic precort," croaked the voice.

"What did he say?" asked the King.

"I haven't a clue. Too much smoke 'em up plant, I suspect."

"Smoke 'em up plant?"

"Here Explorers believe it a harmless herbal weed smoked to enhance visions, meaning, and experiences.

However, in the Maintainers' Guildhall it's an illegal drug held responsible for all manner of wrongdoings."

As they reached the front door Lady Elizabeth said, "Well, that's typical for Explorers. No one home. We'll just have to go to plan two."

"Which is?"

"Hunt them down. The Benevolent Ruler may very well be over at the Royal Treasury office, whereas the Bishop is often at the Temple. Who knows where the Discoverer might be, but perhaps we'll get lucky and find him."

There were places the King had never been in his own kingdom, and the Royal Treasury was one of them. He was interested to see how many people worked in a single large room. Each with their own stool, small desk, ledger, and quill pen, entering rows of figures in the account books.

"I thought this place would have only Maintainers," said the King as they moved along the rows of desks.

"Not at all," said Lady Elizabeth. "You'll find all sorts of people here, as you will in any job. Ah, there she is, our Benevolent Ruler."

The King looked at the person Lady Elizabeth was pointing at. He didn't know what he'd been expecting,

BENEVOLENT RULER

but it wasn't this. She was twenty, at most, bright eyed, and had long raven black hair. As they approached, she glanced up and said, "Lady Elizabeth! Good to see you again." Introductions finished, the King said, "This doesn't look like much of a place for a Benevolent Ruler to do benevolent ruling."

"It's perfect," said the Benevolent Ruler. "I've got everything I need to do my best work. I've got a group of people, everyone in this room, accountants and tax collectors, reporting to me, and I've got a vision of how to make this place better. To top it off, I can step in to remedy the situation when the boss forgets, or neglects, important projects. Before Kingdomality, that would get me in trouble. Now I get thanks." The Benevolent Ruler beamed. "Your timing is perfect. It's nearly the end of the day and we're about to hold our weekly team meeting. Why don't you sit in?"

The King and Lady Elizabeth went to the far side of the room and the Benevolent Ruler announced in a loud voice that it was time to start. Stools and desks were quickly pushed aside and the group gathered around the Benevolent Ruler in the now-open space on the other side of the room.

The Benevolent Ruler began the meeting with a review of that week's production compared to the previous week. Auditors, who watched spending in other royal departments, also gave reports. Several new regulations concerning tax matters were announced and some discussion followed on the problem of how to properly tax bushel baskets of wheat. Wheat for flour, it seemed, was taxed, whereas seed wheat was not.

At the end of the meeting the Benevolent Ruler spoke. Quietly at first, and then with increasing passion, she described her vision to make the Royal Treasury something they'd all be proud of and explained to her staff the key role they all had to play in improving the quality of life for everyone. Roads, hospitals, the military, irrigation canals, the sheriff's office, the foresters, indeed, the future of the whole Kingdom depended upon an effective treasury department. She concluded by telling everyone of the new vision the medical staff had for the hospital and the kingdom's health care system. She said she was totally in support of the vision and made clear the changes the Royal Treasury would be making to fund this vision.

She was a dynamic and persuasive speaker, and the King found himself nodding in agreement. However, first one person, and then several other members of her staff, weren't convinced by the Benevolent Ruler's rhetoric. At first they just shook their heads in disagreement. Then they voiced opposition. "Can't be done" and "Won't work" were two loud comments. The Benevolent Ruler continued on, but at the end of the meeting, as everyone was leaving, she asked Walter, the main objector, to remain for a discussion.

The King expected fireworks. He wouldn't have tolerated that sort of public opposition. But the King was surprised at how calmly the Benevolent Ruler carefully reviewed all she had said. Walter said the money wasn't available and couldn't be raised. The result would be chaos in the health care system and things, while not perfect, would be better left alone. The Benevolent Ruler said sometimes chaos was the price of progress and the money could certainly be raised with little discomfort. Walter continued to disagree and said it wouldn't work. Plus, he claimed, it would be far too disruptive to the health care system.

Most of the others had left when the Benevolent Ruler walked Walter to the door. "My dear Walter, I am sorry we see things differently, but Kingdomality teaches the value of another's opinions. I'll be giving every consideration to your thoughts."

The Benevolent Ruler watched Walter exit and go down the staircase before turning to a trusted aide and saying, "Walter is history. Clean out his desk and send word that he's finished here."

With that, the Benevolent Ruler swept out of the room without saying good-bye.

"Tough lady," said the King. "Reminds me of my mother!"

"Too right," said Lady Elizabeth. "She's tried to work with Walter before, though, to no avail. At some point Benevolent Rulers draw the line. But don't get caught up in how tough a Benevolent Ruler can be if they think it necessary to further the vision. Focus on the vision itself. What did you think of her speech?"

"Incredible," said the King. "That hospital vision is exciting and from what I heard several people say as they left, just what this Kingdom needs. However, I suspect Walter is right. It could lead to chaos—if she pulls it off!"

"I agree," said Lady Elizabeth. "And Explorers prefer chaos to doing nothing. Stirring the pot may mean she has her hands full for a while, but Benevolent Rulers enjoy every minute of it."

As they left the Royal Treasury building, the King said to Lady Elizabeth, "I was surprised to find that the Benevolent Ruler wasn't the King of this Kingdom."

"Could be, of course," said Lady Elizabeth. "But any of the twelve roles can be King or Queen. Royalty or not, though, Benevolent Rulers always find a group to lead. They are the charismatic leaders of the Kingdom. Their natural affinity for human connections and their focus on future possibilities make them the social activists in the Kingdom. They are concerned about the health and well-being of their people, and like all Explorers, they tend to focus on the future, not today."

"So the group they lead doesn't have to be the whole kingdom? It can just be some group at work?" said the King.

"Work, home, Temple, sports field, wherever— Benevolent Rulers find a group to lead, just as Kingdomality Shepherds find a flock to look after. Benevolent Rulers are creatively emotional, though, while Shepherds, you'll remember, are emotionally realistic. They both care about people, but each has a different approach."

"Bishop next?" asked the King.

"That's the plan. Let's check the Palmic temple."

The King followed the Ralcoric system of belief but was familiar with the Palmic faith, based on the divinity of opposable thumbs. Thumbs were held to be sacred and god was thought to be two gigantic thumbs dwelling in a heaven populated by angel fingers.

The Palmics' main religious writings were gathered in a book called *Rule of Thumbs*. Two thumbs up was universally held to be a holy gesture. On the other hand, anyone wanting to snub another person would "thumb their nose" at him or her, and throughout the land the injunction to "put a thumb in it" was understood to be a wish for peace and good health. Adherents of the Palmic faith, when meeting, hooked thumbs and shook thumbs, much as others shake hands.

The King discovered, as they entered the Palmic temple, that the altar rock was a realistic thumb sculpted out of pink marble. Beside the altar sat the Bishop, in long robes. An official of some sort was making an announcement. A commission was about to report to the Bishop. The official announced that three members had sided with the church, while a fourth had supported the state. The matter would now be decided by the Bishop. The issue, the King noted with interest, had to do with the division of powers between church and state.

The King, Lady Elizabeth, and the Wizard sat down in a pew to watch.

When the four commissioners came forward, three stood together while the fourth stood to the other side. The Bishop began by asking each side questions, and the King was interested to see that it was impossible to tell what the Bishop thought. His questions to both sides were tough and pointed.

In summation, the lone commissioner supporting the state's position said, "The matter is really simple, Your Grace. The facts show they are wrong."

"Really? These facts of yours," said the Bishop with a dismissive wave of his hand, "hardly seem relevant to me."

"But, Your Grace, they are specific and focused on this very issue. They speak for themselves."

"Not to me they don't," said the Bishop. "When you've sat on the Throne of Thumbs as long as I have, you learn that facts are but the data being put forward at the moment. No more reliable than a passing cloud. Today this fact, tomorrow another. The facts of men are the whimsy of Big Thick Thumbs, I assure you. That said, I must say I do agree with your position."

"Your Grace!" cried out the three others in alarm. "Agree with his position! We speak for Palmics of record and must protest. Our position is the only one that can resolve the issue."

"You're quite right," said the Bishop, and before the lone man could protest this apparent change he said, "I have spoken. I agree with your position," he said with a nod to the lone commissioner, "and I recognize that you are right," he added with a nod to the three. "I hereby discharge you from the temple and require you all to appear before me in one week with your plan for exactly how you will implement my ruling."

"What ruling?" the King whispered to Lady Elizabeth.

"A typical Bishop one. Unencumbered by the facts, and without seeming aware of the contradiction, the ruling professes two mutually exclusive ideas," replied Lady Elizabeth. "What to others is chameleon-like behavior, and sometimes a paradoxical view, is to a Bishop simply a creative approach to facts. Facts a Maintainer sees as beautiful and enduring are, to Explorers and Bishops in particular, pieces of a puzzle to be used, moved around, or ignored as may best suit the moment. Bishops have few strong attachments to ideas; expediency is their goal."

"What are those people to do?" wondered the King. "They have no idea of what the Bishop wants."

"Again, a typical Bishop approach. Bishops rarely state their goals. Bishops like to slip and slide where they see opportunity. If a Bishop was explicit about what he wanted, he might discover he'd made a political blunder. You don't ascend to the Throne of Thumbs making political blunders. Bishops are master politicians."

While the King and Lady Elizabeth spoke quietly, the Bishop rose from his throne and went over to the altar. There he began recitation of a prayer from a book lying on the altar. When he needed to turn a page, he did so with his thumb.

"They call this 'thumbing through' the prayer book. He could be at it for hours," said Lady Elizabeth. "Bishops in prayer or meditation see visions of the future. These visions drive them to try to change people and circumstances to either avoid, or embrace, the future they've seen.

"Some people think that Bishops are old fuddy duddies, stuck on the past and resistant to change. But that's not really true. Maintainers like things to remain the same because they put a high value on reliability. Bishops prefer possibility to the reliability of tried and true. Bishops cling only to beliefs and rituals, policies and procedures, that enhance holding onto the faithful or converting new adherents. Remember, a Bishop's main focus is on their vision of the future, and to support this vision, Bishops love to see people and circumstances change to bring more believers into the fold. Change now to secure future possibilities! That's the Bishop's rallying cry."

The King said, "My Ralcoric Bishop is always talking about the future too. Other citizens make suggestions, plead, or even demand. My Bishop *tells* me what to do and then threatens me with something awful if I don't. An afterlife in a burning, fiery swamp and being bitten by poisonous toads is one of his favorite threats."

"Effective too, I bet," replied Lady Elizabeth. "Bishops are very good at knowing what motivates people and knowing what strings to pull."

*In modern-day organizations Bishops are
also very good at knowing what strings to pull.*

Others might accuse them of being manipulative, or stooping to threats to get their way. Bishops do not see this as a negative. The possibilities they can see are so important, so worthy, that the ends more than justify the means. Besides, such tactics are not needed with their loyal followers and are reserved for those outside the fold in the hope of bringing them inside. Bishops command respect and even awe from their followers. Bishops can see possibilities. They can manipulate the reality around them so that they make the unreal seem real. This is what makes them successful politicians. Bishops are comfortable being in two places at the same time, be it the present and the future or on both sides of a fence. They are comfortable with ambiguity and can live with a level of uncertainty that might paralyze others. By not being committed to a specific idea or agenda, Bishops in organizations are able to move quickly to take advantage of whatever might come along that can help them foster the change necessary to bring about the future they see.

"Let's get out of here," said the King. Lady Elizabeth nodded agreement and they slipped out the side door.

"Your Ralcoric blood uncomfortable around a Palmic Bishop?" asked Lady Elizabeth.

"Not at all," replied the King. "That Palmic Bishop is the double of the Ralcoric Bishop I have to deal with. And every time I do, I realize sometime later I've been outmaneuvered. That's what makes me uncomfortable."

"Tough adversary," agreed Lady Elizabeth. "Like I said, Bishops have visions of other lives. They're seers and futurists with very creative imaginations. They can see present lives, future lives, and past lives all at the same time. They can hold two opposing views in their heads with equal respect for each being the truth. This may lead some to think them crazy, but they see it as a mark of how shrewd they are."

"Where to now?" asked the King.

"Don't know," said Lady Elizabeth. "Hard to know where the Discoverer might be. One thing about Discoverers is that they're usually off out of the Kingdom discovering."

DISCOVERER

"What do they discover?" asked the King.

"Everything! They always find an idea or an object of value."

"They'd be heroes when they return, then," said the King.

"Not exactly. One of two things generally happens on their return," replied Lady Elizabeth. "First, people may ask 'what use is it?' The Discoverer will then either give a rapid-fire explanation without a great deal of substance or a very detailed explanation that is boring! Either way, the Discoverer's finds aren't usually hailed and adopted in the Kingdom. But he hardly notices. By then he's been hit by the wanderlust and he's long gone."

Lady Elizabeth paused and the King prompted, "You said there were two things?"

"Ah yes. The second thing that can happen is that the locks to the Kingdom get changed and they don't have a key. When the locksmith rekeys, people forget the Discoverer and don't cut him a key. The big challenge for Discoverers is to slow down and stay home long enough to help others understand the innovative idea, or how to use the new gadget. Otherwise, they're in danger of being excluded. It's tough for them to hang around, though. Nobody gets bored faster than a Discoverer. They know the difference between being dead and alive is change. No breath, no heartbeat, no change: dead! Therefore, they think the more change they experience, the more alive they are. They like to lead the way and they have bold confidence in their decisions, and that confidence prompts a decisive approach to life and its challenges."

The King looked at Lady Elizabeth and said, "I notice you've told me far more about the Explorer roles than you did any of the others. How come?"

"Well, the Benevolent Ruler was the only Explorer we actually spoke to and not much more than hello. We didn't speak to the Bishop at all, and I doubt we'll even see the Discoverer. It's best to meet Kingdomality people. But with Explorers that's a tall order, so I need to tell you more about them." Lady Elizabeth spotted someone leaving a small shop. "There's someone who will know if the Discoverer is around. Please, wait here."

Lady Elizabeth was soon back. "As I feared, the Discoverer left earlier this month and, as usual, no one has any idea when he'll be back," she said as she approached with an elderly lady at her side. "We won't be meeting him, but look who I found! Harold, I want you to meet the Discoverer's mother!"

"Charmed, I'm sure," said the King.

"And this is our wizard," said Lady Elizabeth.

"A pleasure," said the Wizard.

"Nice to meet you too," said the Discover's mother. "Please call me Alice."

"I'm sorry we won't meet your son," said the King. "I understand he's difficult to find at home."

"Tell me about it," said the mother. "He breezes in and breezes out before I hardly know he's home. He's a good boy, mind, but not much good when it comes to being reliable. His dad always figured he was absent-minded and flighty. That's not it at all, though. It's just that he sees connections that escape the rest of us. And his mind follows those connections to new things, new ways, new places, new ideas, so fast the rest of us can't follow and think he's a bit daft, but he's not. Not by a long shot."

"She's right, he has had some successes," said Lady Elizabeth.

"Some! I'll say he's had some," said the mother. "All right, all right, I know the wind-driven potato peeler wasn't too practical, and his hot air balloon burned up and will probably never fly, but what about his wool-dying vat? It saves Shepherds a fortune, and my boy was sharp enough to make some gold for himself on that one. Then there's the new mineral he discovered on his last trip that's harder than iron. He had some great ideas about what to do with it, and he's formed a syndicate with the Prime Minister and the Benevolent Ruler to put his ideas to work. Unfortunately, he heard about a new musical instrument in some other Kingdom, so off he went for a look. Of course, if he does find a new way of making music, chances are he'll bring one back with him and he'll be in the music business too."

"Sounds like he's quite the entrepreneur but difficult to pin down," said the King.

"That's my boy, all right. Got more things going than I've got cats in the barn. He's never around when I need him, and if he is around half the time he gets busy with something new and forgets to come to dinner when he's called. All said, though, he's responsible for a lot of the progress in this Kingdom. Who do you think discovered Kingdomality in the first place?"

"You mean . . .?" said the King.

"It wasn't a Dreamer-Minstrel, Black Knight, or Engineer-Builder, that's for sure," said the Discoverer's mother with a fond smile of pride. "Now, I must get home. I never know when that boy is going to show up and be looking for his favorite dish for dinner. Forty-seven days now I've been making dove soup and roasted duck in the afternoon and throwing it out at bedtime, but one of these days he's going to be home, and he's going to be hungry."

The King, Lady Elizabeth, and the Wizard watched her trundle off across the square.

"Only a mother," said the Wizard.

"Pity you've only got one wish to hand out or the King could ask you to produce the Discoverer," said Lady Elizabeth with a smile that suggested she knew more than she was telling.

"Yes, yes, a great shame," said the Wizard quickly.

"It would have been nice," said the King, "but after meeting the mother I feel I know this Discoverer pretty well. I've got a couple just like him in my Kingdom. Matter of fact, I think my own brother must be a Discoverer. He's just like Alice described her son, except he's also very competitive."

"He's a Discoverer for sure then," said Lady Elizabeth. "Now that you know all about Explorers, what can you tell me about them?"

"Well, they're as different from Maintainers as Helpers are from Challengers, that's for sure. Here's my take on Explorers:

· They like change. They stir the pot and don't mind if that means chaos. They believe chaos can lead to improvement, whereas no change equals stagnation, and nothing is worse than stagnation and boredom. And change can lead to the future vison they all see. Explorers are on a lifelong quest to experience new things in new ways.

· Explorers, focused on the future or other worlds, can be out of touch with reality. They can be unrealistic and seem insensitive to others."

· They're possibility thinkers and futurists, visionaries who are happy dwelling in the mists of other worlds, be they parallel, future, or past.

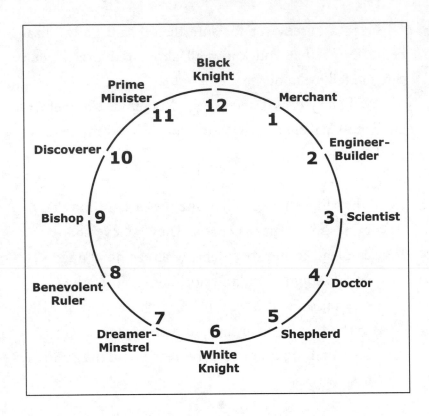

In his mind the King had no trouble seeing the King-domality sundial and updating it to include the Explorers.

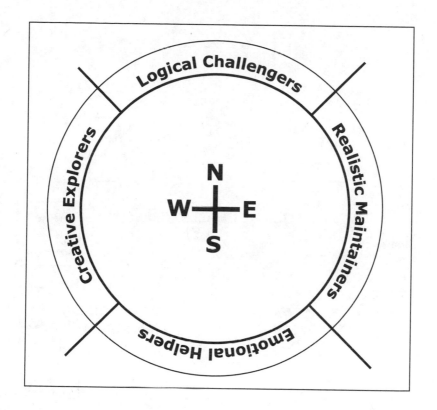

He also had no trouble remembering the framework the twelve roles fit into.

While he needed to remember only Emotional Helpers, Logical Challengers, Realistic Maintainers, and Creative Explorers to put Kingdomality to work, the King had put together his own mind map to include both the four groups and all twelve roles:

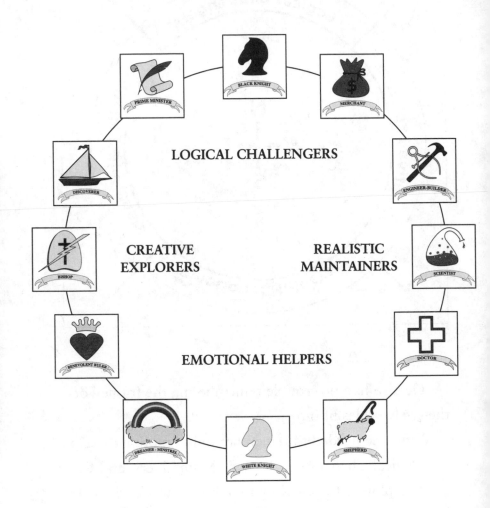

LOGICAL CHALLENGERS

CREATIVE
EXPLORERS

REALISTIC
MAINTAINERS

EMOTIONAL HELPERS

Their business finished, Lady Elizabeth said it was time they were getting home again.

"I'm looking forward to putting Kingdomality to work," said the King. "I need to do some more studying on the twelve roles, but when it comes to the four guildhalls—Helpers', Challengers', Maintainers', and Explorers'—I'm sure I understand them well enough to get started. I'll be a Kingdomality magician!"

Lady Elizabeth said, "Magician work is easy when you know how the trick works. Kingdomality teaches you the secret. It's a guide to understanding how people relate to the world. It gives you basic facts and understandings in a way you can use them. While the magic of the total mind remains a mystery, Kingdomality can reveal enough to help you better utilize people and give you a more effective, productive Kingdom. It won't be magic to you, because you know the secret, but the results can be magical. If you want results, Kingdomality is the way to go!"

Benevolent Rulers, as Lady Elizabeth pointed out, can be found anywhere in the kingdom. And corporate or country, a leader, a King can emerge from any of the four groups with equal ease and success. In recent times such a leader might have defined strong leadership as an excess of his or her own personality, backed by others of a like mind. Today, and in the future, great leaders are, and will be, those who actively seek to temper their own traits and surround themselves with complementary personalities. The lesson of a school suffering from too many Maintainers, and Sir Lockletter's army's troubles because they were short on Maintainers, is no different for Helpers, Challengers, and Explorers. Balance isn't better because it's politically correct, gender neutral, or even nice. Balance is better for the same reason King Harold's army needs foot soldier archers, knights mounted on horses, and catapult launchers riding behind in a wagon. Without all three working together, along with a host of other specialists such as blacksmiths, grooms, cooks, and battering rammers, the army wouldn't win a battle, much less a war. Obvious? Yes. But then take a look at all the organizations where great battering ram bosses keep hiring other battering rammers for every job they can. Challengers hir-

ing Challengers, Helpers hiring Helpers, Maintainers hiring Maintainers, and Explorers hiring Explorers!

IN THE WEST, ON THE LEFT SIDE OF THE SUNDIAL,
ARE THE CREATIVE EXPLORERS.

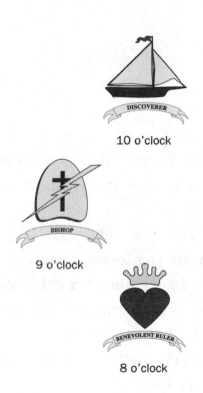

10 o'clock

9 o'clock

8 o'clock

CHAPTER NINE

KINGDOMALITY IN ACTION

*T*HE KING AND LADY ELIZABETH looked around in surprise. They were back in the King's own Throne Room.

"Oops!" said the Wizard. "You did say 'go.' "

"Ah well. Now, how are you feeling about . . . ?" Lady Elizabeth started to ask the King, but a thumping bang on the Throne Room door interrupted. The King's closest adviser, Sir Rodney of Miclamac, entered.

"Disaster, Sire! Absolute disaster!" Sir Rodney wailed.

"What now?" asked the King.

"The new bridge to the west. Westerners are insisting it be made out of a new material called cement. They say it is better than wood. That's what they're claiming: better than wood! Home office is in a tizzy. They don't want wood either. Out east they've got some big boulders they want to use for the foundation. It may take a hundred years to build, but it will last forever. No boulders, no money, they say.

"Meantime, the western construction team decided to get in touch with the soul of the river and sense its essential being so they could ask its permission to build a bridge over it. They've gone off to seek advice from some hermit.

"No sooner were the westerners off to become enlightened than the workers we recruited from the lake district up north packed up and went home when they discovered the bridge was going west. Said it wasn't going to do them any good."

"Let me guess," said the King, breaking into Sir Rodney's lament. "I bet the workers from the south are whipping around giving everybody hugs and trying to bring peace."

Sir Rodney looked close to tears. "That's the way it started. But no one hugged back. The departing westerners might have, I think, but something new caught their interest and suddenly off they went. The north refused flat out. They said hugging didn't make sense and wouldn't solve the cement boulder problem. The eastern office wouldn't let them in—said they were too busy for 'unrealistic touchy-feely hogwash.' Then the southerners got mad, said no one appreciated them, and they were going home too. They left in a huff! It's a disaster, Your Majesty. A total disaster. Who knows if the bridge will ever be finished, much less on time," cried Sir Rodney.

"Of course it will be finished," said the King. "It's just our north-south-east-west-square-peg-in-a-round-hole problem. Now, here's what we're going to do. First thing, we have to get everyone's attention. I want four Royal Proclamations. The first will go to the western work crew and say that Serena the Soothsayer has declared next week the most propitious time to begin construction and a Rite of Relinquishment will be held on Monday, followed by a cookout supper, to mark the commencement of construction."

"What's a Rite of Relinquishment?" asked Sir Rodney.

"Haven't a clue," said the King, "except it's bound to involve incantations to the river's essential being, whatever that is, and incense. Wouldn't hurt to trot out the Runic Bishop, and a Palmic one too if you can find one, to give a blessing. We'd best let them know the bridge is a unique new design that has never been built before. 'Your chance to be part of a fourteenth-century engineering marvel,' would be a good line.

"The second proclamation will go to the eastern office announcing a formal dinner to mark commencement of construction of the bridge approved by the office under funding approval G8894. As for the concrete and boulder issue, the proclamation will say that the eastern end of the bridge will be anchored by boulders and the western by concrete, with ongoing performance to be monitored by the office's research division and a report from the science council to be presented at the annual office convention. A baseline survey, with full eastern crew in attendance, will follow the morning after the dinner.

"The third proclamation, which is for the southern folk, will announce that next week there will be a sod-turning ceremony for the new bridge, at which time a bronze plaque will be unveiled celebrating the contribution of the south to the quality of life in the Kingdom. All bridge workers are to be honored. Then throw in a couple of paragraphs about the urgent need for the bridge so that volunteer firefighters can quickly come to help each other.

"Finally, I want a proclamation to go north. It will announce an on-the-job bridge-building competition with cash prizes for all winners. The competition will be called the International Invitational. Matter of fact, put that right on top and under it the slogan 'The Smart Place to Be.' Across the bottom put 'Go for the Gold.' Invite workers from a couple of other kingdoms and get the word out that out-of-state workers are bragging to the town crier that they'll win every event.

"Don't worry about the bridge, Sir Rodney," concluded the King. "It is going to be built right on schedule, mark my words. Those proclamations will get those workers back and then we'll use the same tactics to keep them focused on bridge building. Exciting new things for the westerners, policies and procedures for the easterners, caring concern and people benefits for my southerners, and a constant challenge and logical reasoning for the folks from the north."

"I like it," said Sir Rodney. "Everybody gets what they want!"

"Actually, everybody gets what they need. It's King-domality in action. And speaking of which, I have a very important job for you, Sir Rodney. I want you to keep track of exactly what's going on at the job site and report to me every Monday morning. Okay?"

Sir Rodney replied, "Oh yes, Sire. A full accounting every Monday."

Bowing low, Sir Rodney marched out of the Throne Room much happier than when he'd arrived.

"I'm pretty sure Rodney's a Maintainer, that's why I gave him the job of keeping track of construction," said the King. "I used to have him working full-time on new policy and initiative development, but I think this will be more to his liking."

"Stroke of genius, Your Majesty," said Lady Elizabeth, for like all smart, successful management consultants, she knew when a dollop of ingratiating praise for having done the obvious was in order.

The King, like all kings, was glad to accept the praise but looked troubled. "I'm able to peg Rodney because he's obviously a Maintainer. But how do I peg people I don't know so well?"

"Excellent question. Here's one way to do it. You can give your people a short eight-question test. Here's a copy of the test and how to score it.[1] But if you want a fast determination, ask the following question:[2]

"In general, how long should a book be? Explorers will assume it's fiction and want to know how good it is. Good books, they think, should go on and on. Maintainers will assume it's nonfiction. They'll tell you it needs to be long enough to give you all the information you need. Helpers won't care if it's fiction or nonfiction, but they'll want to know if the book carries a good message. Good message books can be long ones. Like Helpers, Challengers won't care if it's fiction or nonfiction, but they'll tell you how much time they have to read it."

No sooner had Lady Elizabeth finished than the Throne Room door again swung open, this time to admit Lincoln of Lanslow, the King's Loyal Sergeant of the Chamber.

---

1. If you haven't already done so, on page 00 you will find a test that will tell you which of the four groups you belong to. Or you can let your computer do some more complex calculating by taking a simple, eight-question, multiple-choice test at *www.kingdomality.com* that will pin down your actual Kingdomality role.

2. In an organization, asking someone how much time they have to meet with you will result in Maintainers saying "whatever's needed," Helpers "all you want," Explorers will want to know how interesting the subject is before answering, and Challengers will give you "X" minutes.

"Your Majesty," began the Loyal Sergeant of the Chamber. Before he could go any further, though, the King said, "Sergeant, I'd like your thoughts on this: In general, how long should a book be?"

"Depends on what it's about, I should imagine. I'd not want to waste the paper if it wasn't a worthwhile book."

"Worthwhile? You mean a book with a good message?"

"That's it."

"Well then, Lincoln of Lanslow, I could use your help. I've got some people who need you. Let me introduce you," said the King, putting his arm over Lincoln of Lanslow's shoulders and leading him out the door.

The King's voice faded as he left the Throne Room and Lady Elizabeth, turning to the Wizard, said, "This King really *is* going to set the world on fire!"

"Absolutely," said the Wizard.

His remark really wasn't needed, except it is common knowledge, or at least it was in the time of which we speak, that Wizards always had the last word.

AUTHORS' CONCLUDING COMMENTS

Lady Elizabeth and the Wizard were right. Unprecedented prosperity came to the Kingdom. Families, schools, trade guilds, and even the military used Kingdomality.

Rather than being grumpy, out-of-sorts, quarrelsome, and defeatist, the King's subjects became happy, in tune, cooperative, and positive. As Kingdomality changed the way they worked, and began to produce better results, their attitude also improved and so results improved, which improved attitude, which improved results.

Some found whole new lines of work more suited to their natural talents. Chopper Charles, the King's executioner, turned in his blade and opened a store selling formal gowns and imported fashions for ladies. Go figure! Kingdomality provided the new mind-set that allowed people to see things differently and match what they did with what they'd like to do.

Whereas the King had to be content with asking the "How long should a book be?" question, or calculating test results, you can go to www.kingdomality.com and discover exactly what your Kingdomality role is. Thousands of organizations around the world are already using the Kingdomality Web site to discover who they're working with.

Finally, did you notice? A consultant solved the King's problem better than he could have himself! A great relief to the authors, who have

*been known to engage in a bit of Kingdom cor-
rection themselves from time to time. You might
like to look at the Services Available on page
000. Also, we've included a brief guide for readers, "Strokes and Strikes." Strokes and Strikes is
designed to give you a quick thumbnail sketch
of each of the twelve roles and examples of the
sorts of things people in that role would see as a
positive experience (strokes) and things that
would be negative (strikes). Finally, readers
interested in using Kingdomality in organizations will also want to have a look at "A Meeting with King," Peter, on page 000, which tells
of a visit made by our King to learn how King
Peter had actually used Kingdomality to make
his kingdom successful.*

A MEETING WITH KING PETER:

Putting Kingdomality To Work In Your Kingdom

NOT LONG AFTER our King returned home and started to put Kingdomality to work, he had a surprise visit from two old friends, the Wizard and Lady Elizabeth.

"How's it going?" asked the Wizard.

"Pretty tough," answered Lady Elizabeth before the King had a chance to reply.

"So why ask? But, if you must know, it's more difficult than I thought it would be. I'm never quite sure what to do."

"But you have been trying," said Lady Elizabeth, "and that's what counts. It's time we took a trip."

"Back to the Kingdomality Kingdom?" asked the King.

"No, this time you get the real thing. We're going to take you back to Peter's kingdom and you'll actually meet Peter! It's time we boosted your enthusiasm. Nothing like seeing a Kingdomality success to get you excited. Best of all, Peter will tell you his four-step action plan so you can create a Kingdomality success story, just as he has."

"Sounds great! When do we go?" asked the King.

"Silly question," muttered the Wizard.

The King looked down. His red rug had turned blue. His Throne Room was a dinning hall. It wasn't even his castle! Ahead was a formal dining table with a footman behind each chair and at the head . . . yes! King Peter himself. Our King recognized him from a portrait hung in the meeting room at last year's Royal Convention.

"Ah, there you are!" said King Peter. "Have a seat. You must be famished."

"Delighted to be here." The King sat down on Peter's right. Lady Elizabeth sat to Peter's left, while the Wizard sat opposite.

The table was silent as heaping platters of roast venison, potatoes, and corn and a pot of steaming gravy appeared. When each guest had been served, the King asked Peter the secret of his success.

"The secret is Kingdomality," he said.

"I know that," said the King.

"And what does it mean?"

"Well, the four main groups are Helpers, Challengers, Maintainers, and Explorers, each with three personality roles. I've seen eleven of them, all except the Discoverer. But how do I use Kingdomality? How do I actually put it to work?"

"Easy. Just remember you're the king. K.I.N.G. It's an acronym that guides you through the process," said Peter. "The 'K' is for 'Know yourself. Know others.' It all begins with the four main personality groups. Understand what drives you and what drives everyone you work with. Kingdomality is a magic mirror. It shows a reflection of who you and others are. It may not be highly polished and show you everything, but it's sharp enough to help you read people. Kingdomality lets you discover how a particular person is like you and how he or she differs."

"Once you know yourself and know others," said

Lady Elizabeth, "you can do two things. First, communicate effectively. Because you understand what it's like to be in another's shoes, how other persons see the world, you can frame your message so that they really hear what you want them to."

The King smiled. "Nothing to be gained promising a Maintainer an exciting visionary venture filled with new untested ideas as the mantra of the moment, or suggesting to a Challenger the project is a worthy one but has little chance of success and even less of a payoff. I see that."

Lady Elizabeth said, "The second thing you can do better is motivate. Motivation also has to be targeted."

"That was tough for me," said King Peter. "My Kingdomality role is Doctor, and I knew what was important: maintaining the status quo, keeping things orderly, and helping people. I never questioned that what motivated me would motivate everyone else. It took me some time to understand that not only did others see things from a different perspective, but that their perspective was a valid one.

"Knowing who you are, and who your people are, allows you to communicate a specific plan or idea to a targeted audience and then motivate those people to take action."

"Powerful," said the King with obvious respect.

Peter's next lesson was also powerful.

"The 'I' in K.I.N.G. stands for *'Identify the issues.'* You need to develop two clear statements," said Peter. "First, what's the present situation? What's happening now? You need the views of Helpers, Explorers, Challengers, and Maintainers, if not every personality type within the four groups, to see that clearly. Second, what's better? Again, you need input from all points on the Kingdomality compass. A problem or opportunity exists only when you can identify the difference between the first and second. If you can't set out both what's happening now and what would be better, all you've got is a meaningless grump about today or pie-in-the-sky thinking about tomorrow."

"Next is the 'N' in K.I.N.G.," said Lady Elizabeth. "The 'N' stands for *'Name your team.'* Once you have identified the issue and know yourself and others, then you're in a position to create a team that can be effective. Or, select a single person. The difference between Kingdomality and what you're doing now is that you're digging down deeper, discovering another layer of a person's ability to achieve success with a particular project."

"It's no big mystery," interjected King Peter. "You match skill and work, right? A literate person to head the Royal Library, for example. For your army you want someone who knows military tactics. So, why would you put a literate Explorer in charge of the library, or a Maintainer military tactic expert in charge of the army?"

"Because I wanted the Explorer to expand the library into new areas and the Maintainer to instill a sense of tradition and loyalty in the army?" asked the King.

"You've got it," said Peter. "You've matched the issue to a personality group for a specific desired result. Before I learned about Kingdomality role types and their preferences, I'd never have made an appointment without assessing traditional skills and abilities. Now, I also always do a Kingdomality assessment. Skills tell you if they can do the job; preferences can tell you something about the way they're likely to do it and how they'll work with others to get it done."

"Finally we have the 'G' in K.I.N.G.," said Lady Elizabeth. "The 'G' stands for *Get goals and get going!* When you know yourself and know others, have identified the issue, and matched people to tasks—based on their Kingdomality role, as well as skill and ability— you need to set goals. The 'get going' is a reminder that, until you do, all your Kingdomality preparation doesn't amount to a hill of beans. But first, you have to set goals."

King Peter said, "And these goals are implementation goals. Goals that are the necessary next steps to reach that state we called 'what's better' when we were identifying issues."

Lady Elizabeth said, "Finally 'get going' reminds you to push on. In some Kingdoms the getting-ready-to-go-to-work phase of a project can go on, and on, and on. It's what Kings do. You've heard it said that 'good enough is never good enough'? Well, sometimes the fact is that 'good enough is as good as you need' and it's time to get going!"

"That's it, then. Know yourself, know others. Identify the issues. Name your team. Get goals and get going. K.I.N.G. Put that to work in your Kingdom and you'll soon be fending off speaking invitations from the Royalty Convention," said Peter.

"I have a little gift for you," said Peter and he handed the King a gold box. On the lid was an engraved silver plate that read:

K   Know yourself. Know others.

I   Identify the issues.

N   Name your team.

G   Get goals and get going.

"All you have to do is follow what it says on the lid and you'll soon be able to fill it with jewels," said Peter.

"Well, there are several other important things," said Lady Elizabeth. "Establishing deadlines, measuring performance, skill training, and setting up a system of reward and recognition—being careful, of course, to reward the right things in the right way, not just handing out gold from the Royal Treasury willy-nilly."

"She's teasing me," said King Peter as he led them out of the dining room. "Before I learned Kingdomality, a rascal management consultant talked me into a reward program that cost me five pounds of gold before I realized what a fraud he was."

"Tsk. Tsk. My goodness, five pounds! Imagine that," said the King, remembering his own ten pounds of gold wasted on a consultant.

"It wasn't one of my best decisions," said King Peter. "The worst part, however, wasn't the five pounds of gold. The worst part was that it blinded me to how important it is to reward performance. Lady Elizabeth taught me reward in the Kingdom needed to be patterned after teaching my son Prince Elrid how to walk."

"Sounds like a strange way to run a Kingdom," said the King.

"I thought so too at first. But it worked with Elrid and it works with anybody. It's called praising. The essence is that when Elrid was learning to walk, I didn't wait until he could walk across a room to praise him. The first time he pulled himself shakily to his feet, I lavished him with praise. I ran to get his mother so she could see Elrid stand! That kind of performance didn't get praised when he was ten, but to start it got me wildly cheering.

"Now, with everyone, I praise progress no matter how small, and as they get better I move the bar. Kingdomality is powerful stuff, all right but if I didn't praise progress, I'd not be much further ahead."

"In the further-ahead department, you're sure beating my Kingdom," said the King. "I'll remember, *get goals and get going*, and I'll praise progress too."

The King looked as if he wanted to say something more but was unsure exactly what, or at least unsure how to word it.

"The Doctor in me tells me you have a problem," said King Peter.

"Not exactly a problem," said the King. "But Kingdomality is a lot of stuff, a lot of ideas to try to put to work."

"It is," said Peter. "Let me give you an example of how it works. We have a good wood industry and some mining. Our markets are the flatland kingdoms, such as yours. Being a Doctor, I knew what our customers wanted. First, do no harm! Then, keep producing the same product, go slow with innovations. Sales were handled by a central selling agency. Very convenient. For a Maintainer-Doctor, that is. I could divide sales amongst the various woodcutters and miners. It was a great system. Or at least I thought it was.

"With Kingdomality I was pushed by Explorers to look at new products and innovations, ways we could add value to timber and minerals. Challengers had some interesting and, I felt, alarming ideas about how we could charge more and deliver faster while improving our product. Helpers helped me see that if I was willing to trade a little structure for spontaneity to satisfy Explorers, and trade a little status quo protection for improvement to satisfy Challengers, I'd be able to find a different, more balanced answer to the 'what's better' question. Helpers also showed me that forest workers and miners were better suited and would be happier selling their own products than going through a central agency because they knew all about their products and enjoyed telling customers about them. That led me to recognize other issues and to reshuffle priorities. Better decision making, starting with decentralized sales, led to better results."

"Yes, I can see how that would work," said the King.

"It worked for me, all right," said Peter. "We'd always thought a customer was a customer. But not so.

"Our Challenger customers were looking for logical reasons to buy our timber or minerals. Now we can talk to them about different grades and types of timber for different uses and how they can logically use our minerals in specific combinations to suit their needs. We might be more expensive than the competition, but you can bet when we talk to a Challenger customer we have a logical reason for that.

"For Explorer customers we try to keep up a constant stream of creative new ideas. We provide something new for the Explorer to be part of. Even a new delivery system can get Explorers excited to see if it will be better.

"We show our Helper customers how using our timber and minerals is going to make life better for people. We used to sell a thirty-foot-long oak beam and the only question we'd ask was how thick did they want it. Now we sell our farm-to-market bridge package designed to provide fresher produce to the towns folk and increased revenue to rural residents. We know Helpers make gut decisions and we make sure they have a good feel about what we're selling them.

"Maintainer customers are different again. Take that same bridge package. We might sell it to an Explorer as opening a new route, to a Helper as benefiting quality of life, and to a Challenger as the logical way to connect two trade roads. To Maintainers we talk about keeping traditional trading relationships open and maintaining infrastructure. Maintainers love the word 'infrastructure.' And 'maintaining infrastructure' is a magic phrase."

"Lady Elizabeth told me that Kingdomality may not be magic but the results can be magical. I can see why," said the King.

"It's true," said King Peter. "I've oversimplified in my example, of course, but at the same time, it really is that simple. Once you know the four main groups and work with K.I.N.G. for a while, it becomes easy. You start out very much in control, but as you determine the preferences in others and learn where your own preferences lie, you'll begin to relinquish control.

"In time you'll find you trust others, who are very different from you and think differently, to make better decisions than you do in some sorts of matters. For example, when you're sick, really sick, do you decide what medicine to take or do you leave that to your doctor?"

"The doctor, of course," said the King.

"And the reason is trust. You trust him to make a better decision than you can for three reasons: training, knowledge, and experience. You'll find you develop a similar trust, in some matters, with others who belong to a different Kingdomality group than your own.

"When you first get started, you're going to have attacks of the 'but-I'm-King' syndrome and you'll want to take back decision making and make all decisions yourself. But unless you're as thick as a post, you'll also begin to realize that your job as king isn't to make all the decisions. Your job, as king, is to decide who the decision makers are going to be in each situation and make changes when necessary. It's a much higher form of kingship and one you'll find comes easy."

"I could use a little 'easy' in my Kingdom," said the King.

He nodded thoughtfully as he considered all King Peter had said while Lady Elizabeth began to say their good-byes. "It's time we were off. I do want to thank you for . . ."

"Yes, off!" exclaimed the Wizard for no better reason than once again getting in the last word!

STROKES AND STRIKES:

A Kingdomality Guide to Dealing with People

*T*HE FOLLOWING IS A quick reference to the twelve Kingdomality roles, presented in the order you met them.

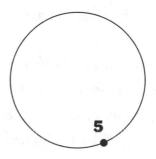

STROKES

· Cooperation and camaraderie
· Valuable relationships
· Structured, warm environment

STRIKES

· Having to enforce rules

· Traitors
· Harsh criticism

Shepherds are the nicest people in the Kingdom. They tend to be consistent in their behavior toward others. Best of all, perhaps, they are glad to talk and share, and they listen because they are always genuinely interested in both the person and the topic. The overriding goal of Shepherds is to tend their flock. They understand the needs of those for whom they are responsible; they are vigilant, reliable, and dependable and engender a feeling of trust, comfort, and stability in those within their charge. Shepherds recognize their obligation to the well-being of those entrusted to their care and are committed caregivers. On the positive side, Shepherds can be empathic, caring, understanding, practical, and realistic. Their deep conviction that they know what is best for those around them can lead a Shepherd to use any manner of inducement to get their flock to conform to their wishes. They know that for the good of the group, sometimes individual members need to be culled, or if a wolf can't be frightened off, it must be eliminated. A Shepherd's singlemindedness of purpose can sometimes be interpreted as manipulative and rigid. Shepherds care what others think of them and can take criticism personally.

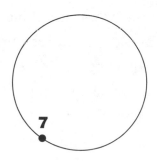

STROKES

· Motivating others
· Meeting new people
· Having fun

STRIKES

· A solitary environment
· Lots of details
· Cutthroat competition

Dreamer-Minstrels are the most charismatic individuals in the Kingdom. They have the ability to get people elated and are the public relations people of the Kingdom. They enjoy traveling around and telling the villagers about their wonderful Kingdom. The Dreamer-Minstrel will find the silver lining in any situation and the pot of gold at the end of every rainbow. It was a Dreamer-Minstrel who, upon finding a pile of manure under the Christmas tree, ran excitedly around the house looking for the pony Santa had left. They have the capacity to build tremendous teams and to get people excited about all manner of things—nearly as excited as they get themselves! Dreamer-Minstrels travel throughout the land spinning tales of great delight and positive imagery. They are the poetic optimists of the Kingdom, who may take a bit of poetic license with the facts. They are eternal optimists, offering encouragement, support, and hope for a better tomorrow. Everything has its season and purpose to Dreamer-Minstrels, and "everything will work out for the best" is their philosophy. As the name implies, they are often creative but many times can be impractical dreamers. When not excitedly beating the public relations drum for some cause or other, Dreamer-Minstrels can be found sitting at the side of the road gazing vacantly, hour after hour, watching the grass grow and an occasional mouse or squirrel scamper by.

White Knights are the heroes of the Kingdom. They believe and fight for the cause as long as they perceive this cause to be good and just. They want to fight on the "right" side. Although they have weapons, they do not like to kill, take no pleasure in it, but they will kill if necessary to help their cause. White Knights are also the crusaders of the Kingdom. They are natural strategists who enjoy the challenge of fighting the good fight. They are the seekers of the Holy Grail. They are the

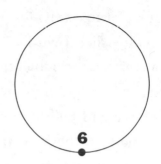

STROKES

· A crusade
· Recognition
· Ideas and principles

STRIKES

· Shallow values
· Unfeeling obstructionists
· Mercenaries

idealists who will charge off into battle to elevate the downtrodden and lift up the masses. They have an affinity for "causes" and will endure many hardships fighting for their ideals. Like Don Quixote, they "dream the impossible dream and fight the unbeatable foe" on a routine basis. The more forbiding the challenge, the more enticing it is to a White Knight. Unfortunately, these fearless warriors do wear out! When they do, their demise is a dramatic and heroic one. Having experienced the exhilaration of victory and then plumbed the depths of despair, they whither and succumb. White Knights can see themselves as martyrs:

long-suffering individuals who endure much so others can enjoy their own lives, undisturbed by the weighty concerns that trouble the White Knight. Once they reach their maximum, however, they no longer suffer in silence and will loudly point out the sacrifices they have made in the hope of being acknowledged. White Knights have a deep need to be appreciated and praised by those around them.

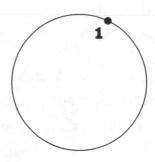

STROKES

· Make and close a deal
· Calculate realistic potential of a deal
· Construct a logically sound transaction

STRIKES

· Being rushed to a decision
· An ill-conceived plan

· Not having all the details

Merchants are the bottom-line people of the Kingdom. They are very meticulous, think things through carefully, and are the most considered decision makers. Merchants like to make perfect decisions and love to perfect whatever they are working on. Good enough doesn't apply to them! Merchants require time to ponder and calculate all the implications of a potential transaction. They are the no-nonsense types that value common sense, consistency, and reliability. Even when convinced of the wisdom of a course of action, Merchants will continually assess their position to monitor the changing risks and rewards. They like to keep their options open so they can continue to act to maximize reward and minimize risk as conditions change. Merchants hold nothing to be absolute. They rely on reasoning and insight to provide the edge they seek in all interactions.

Prime Ministers are the power behind the throne. Prime Ministers will pitch in themselves to get whatever needs to be done finished, in addition to helping form the vision and develop the strategy. Warning: Never tell them how to do things. Their attitude is, "There are many problems in the Kingdom . . . none in my area."

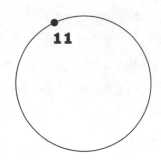

STROKES

· Power
· Getting results
· A winning strategy

STRIKES

· Being put in the spotlight
· Ineptitude of others
· Wasting time

Their focus is on productivity and the end result. Others can find them very direct, at times even blunt. Prime Ministers are, and see themselves as, the true source of power in the Kingdom. Frequently they will work in the background, as they often prefer to shun the spotlight so they can carry out their deals with minimum scrutiny and interference. Prime Ministers are excellent logicians and exceptional strategists. They are results oriented and scrupulously efficient.

Black Knights are the warriors of the realm. Everything is a battle to a Black Knight, and "to the victor go

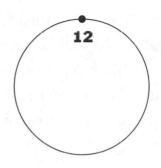

STROKES

· Winning
· Receiving commensurate
  rewards
· Being master of own fate

STRIKES

· Losing
· Not being rewarded
· Ill-conceived campaigns

the spoils." If they think the reward is diminishing or disappearing, they will quickly seek another project, another battle. Black Knights are persuasive, charismatic, and logical. They formulate solid strategies and effectively use their skills to engage others and enlist them on their team. Black Knights are cunning warriors who continuously conduct risk-reward analyses and who are willing to use their weapons if need be. Black Knights see themselves as beneficent free agents whose efforts create bounty for their followers and allies.

"What's good for a Black Knight is good for the Kingdom" could well be their motto. What others see as tough, Black Knights see as realistic. Black Knights tend to be out front and in your face. No artifice. No playing games for the fun of it. Games and life are serious business.

Doctors are the committed professionals: They tend to the needs of people in the Kingdom. They are calm and courteous. The best way to understand a doctor is to understand the most obvious way of upsetting them:

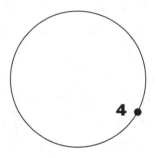

STROKES

· Have a mission/purpose
· Solid procedures

· Realistic structure

STRIKES

· Chaos and disorder
· Wild or irresponsible experimentation
· Impatience and foolhardiness

skipping a hierarchal level or disregarding the steps in an established process. They may appear slightly stubborn, but only because they believe that what they are doing is serious business. Others can see them as detached because they prefer to step back from confrontations, since they don't want others to be upset or emotional. Doctors approach their work with a sense of mission and purpose. They are known for their ability to listen carefully, identify problems, and offer solid practical advice. They like systems and see the world as a place where order and reason should prevail over chaos. They are inspired by the struggle against the dark forces of disease and malignancy throughout the Kingdom. Doctors constantly focus on improving their techniques, increasing their knowledge, and perfecting procedures. They search tirelessly for the "one best way" and work tirelessly to that end, but always by using standardized and recognized processes. They are not given to wild experimentation and see the advancement of knowledge as an orderly progression rather than an explosive enlightenment. Doctors are quite resistant to change. New ideas must be thoroughly proven before they will be adopted.

Engineer-Builders are very solid citizens as well as the perfectionists of the Kingdom. Once they are set in a par-

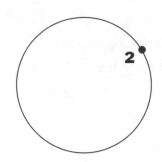

STROKES

· Apply technology to
· Getting the job done
· Providing structure

STRIKES

· Extraneous issues
· Ambiguity
· Inconsistencies and
  improper reasoning

ticular direction, powerful forces and arguments are needed to get them to change. Engineer-Builders don't want to be responsible for a mistake, and changes in direction often equate with changes in proven approaches. They are most comfortable in a stable, structured environment. They provide structure to the Kingdom as they erect the walls that protect and build the roads that ease the way. Engineer-Builders virtually define the realm. They can be seen about the Kingdom measuring, hammering, clearing the land, and building shelters, shops, and castles. They are also inventors of labor-saving devices who provide the subjects of the realm with all manner of clever devices to accomplish their tasks. They have a no-nonsense, straightforward approach to resolving problems and they enjoy their practical approach to problem solving. Engineer-Builders like to see the results of their work. They have a low tolerance for ambiguity and political wrangling while favoring precision and exactitude. They want the freedom to build without having to deal with extraneous issues. They have a talent for spotting inconsistencies and improper reasoning, with little patience for those who choose to diverge from the tried and true path.

Deep in the castle, through a labyrinth of stairs, corridors, and doors, Scientists contentedly mix and blend in their search for true knowledge. The quest is pure and thrilling for curious Scientists, since they use their knowledge to glean deeper understanding of the world in which they live. They are dogmatic in their pursuit. They will countenance no heretical notions or statements in their orderly world. Scientists are the careful assemblers of facts. Their major joy in life is to be left undisturbed to develop, analyze, and critique new ideas. They treat all data as potential treasure to be noted and carefully preserved for probable future value. Scientists' need for order can sometimes cause them not to recog-

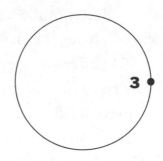

STROKES

· To search for knowledge
· To analyze and critique
· To be the keeper
  of knowledge

STRIKES

· Heretics
· Speculation
· Disorder

nize the facts if the facts do not fit neatly into their plan. They will overlook information that contradicts deeply held beliefs. They are not particularly good at pure speculation, or hypothesizing, because their minds attend only to what is known, not to what is unknown. Scientists are noted for their exceptional analytical skills, not their people skills. They can be perceived as rude, brusque, and uncaring when, in fact, they are totally unaware that others view them as such. Whereas others engage in social niceties, Scientists are busy thinking other thoughts, spaced out, if you will. Their intellect

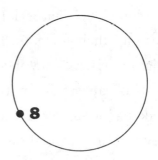

STROKES

· Sharing their vision
  with others
· An appreciative
  audience
· Loyal followers

STRIKES

· Doubt their vision

· Question their
  leadership
· Lack of commitment
  to others

and curiosity are both a curse and blessing to the Scientist, providing solace and imprisonment at the same time.

Benevolent Rulers are the visionaries of the Kingdom. They are driven to share their vision with all in the realm and are the magnetic and powerful leaders of the Kingdom. They are concerned about their subjects and truly believe their vision is best for all. They see commitment in the struggle. Benevolent Rulers are deeply committed to correcting the social ills in the

Kingdom. Their natural affinity toward human connections and their focus on future possibilities make them social activists. Benevolent Rulers are charismatic leaders who can stand on the balcony of the castle and speak passionately of their vision for a better world. They not only care about their subjects; they yearn for, and require, reciprocal feelings. They see nobility in all people and have a fondness for the simple pleasures of life. Because Benevolent Rulers are future oriented, they tend to focus not on the current circumstances but on the potential changes and improvements just waiting to be made. They look forward to the positive results of their visions and enjoy sharing their plans with others.

Bishops have a very complex and demanding role in the Kingdom. They are both religious (propounders of the profound and mystic truths that transcend physical reality) and political (concerned with the practical affairs of the state/organization/family and its citizens/employees/members). Bishops nimbly navigate the dangerous waters when the affairs of Church (other-world mystical) and State (nuts-and-bolts realistic) cross. Bishops are known for their masterful political plotting and can be very convincing and persuasive. They have an uncanny ability to feel comfortable on either side of an argument without

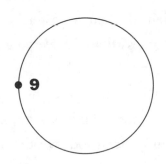

STROKES	STRIKES
· Giving opinions	· Lack faith in their concepts
· Leading a discussion	· Question the validity of their ideas
· Brainstorming ideas	· Challenge their facts

feeling less committed to either side. They seem to be inherently creative with reality and "facts." Bishops are comfortable with ambiguity, since facts are nothing more than the information being currently examined. Bishops have a talent for bringing their vision to life and making the unreal real. Intuitive strategists, Bishops are bold leaders who hold mighty sway over the hearts and minds of all. Beware of a Bishop's wrath—It is mercurial and far reaching. Bishops require unflagging loyalty and frequently test their associates' faithfulness so they can be reassured of the extent of their followers' commitment. If they sense anything less than unswerving faith, an Inquisition is sure to follow.

Discoverers are the entrepreneurs of the Kingdom. They are influential but not necessarily embraced or even understood by others, since they tend to march to their own drummer. Discoverers have the potential to convince a Prime Minister, a Benevolent Ruler, or even a

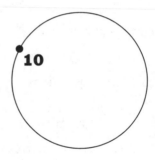

STROKES

· New people, places, things
· Try something new or different

STRIKES

· Have to repeat something
· Follow a routine or schedule
· Follow an impulse
· Being boxed in

Dreamer-Minstrel. The overriding goal of Discoverers is in the famous phrase Go where no one has gone before. They are confident and decisive, and can be inspirational leaders. They seek change and their competitive side drives them to be lead dog. Although they are open-minded and just, Discoverers' confidence makes them appear impulsive and, some might feel, arrogant. Discoverers see a smorgasbord of opportunities and many horizons, and are drawn to all, which can make it difficult for them to set priorities or direction and result in procrastination. Being travelers in time, space, and ideas, Discoverers leave the Kingdom—go off on their own—periodically. When they return, they always bring back something of value, although others may have trouble understanding what it is, what it does, or how useful it is. Discoverers need to remember to stay in the Kingdom long enough to help others understand their discovery—be it an object or an innovative idea. When they do take the time, they can be very successful.

THE SECRET TRUTH ABOUT WHITE KNIGHTS, BLACK KNIGHTS, SCIENTISTS, AND BISHOPS

*T*HESE FOUR ROLES might be thought of as the "pure" roles, and because there are far fewer pure types, many personality-profiling systems, which are also based on the pioneering work of Carl Jung, ignore them altogether and create a system based on the eight other roles by identifying which guildhall (basic group) would be their dominant one and which would be the second most attractive to them.

We feel these abbreviated systems lose much of the richness and insight of Jung's work, and we also know from the more than twelve million people who have taken the Kingdomality test at *www.kingdomality.com* that there are indeed a goodly number of Scientists, White Knights, Bishops, and Black Knights out there. These pure types are important in a family or an organization.

For the sake of simplicity, we too have fudged a bit on these four roles and we want to come clean. These four roles are not quite as pure as we present them, as students of Jung's work know full well. Each of these four roles *does* have a secondary characteristic, just as a Shepherd is primarily a Helper and secondly a Maintainer and a Prime Minister is primarily a Challenger and secondly a Discoverer. On the sundial the second personality theme is found in the adjoining guildhall, except for Scientists, White Knights, Bishops, and Black Knights. For these four Kingdomality roles the next closest personality role is found directly across the sundial face. In tough times, when under stress, when all abilities, talents, and skills must be called on, White Knights have Black Knight skills and Scientists have Bishop skills and vice versa.

This may seem strange, but think about it. When pushed, the White Knight has the weapons of a Black Knight and can set aside emotion and rely on logic to tell him or her that the time has come to use these weapons and kill the dragon. The Black Knight may be seeking his own reward but will, if needed, set aside logic and rescue the maiden or kill the dragon because he or she cares about what happens to others, even if they don't get paid this time. The Scientist will hold on to the realistic, slow, tried-and-true approach, but if that fails will call on his creative side to think outside the box and come up with a brilliant new understanding of the world. The Bishop can rein in the creative urge to keep options open and a foot in two camps and summon his or her realistic side to speak firmly in support of a single position.

CREATE A COUNTRY

MOST OF US have thought about that "perfect" place. Many stories have been written about far-away secret lands and Shangri-las where people can realize their hopes, dreams, and ambitions. Create a Country offers you an opportunity to think about and describe what might be the ideal place for you to live, work, and play.

Many people object to simple, multiple-choice tests like the one that follows. And they have valid concerns. We recognize that your present mood will influence your responses. You may appear to be someone for the moment, not typical of who you are, most of the time. Don't worry. Go with your first thought, your instinct. Look at the following clues like a detective examining possibilities, rather than looking for absolutes. There are no wrong answers, just as there are no absolutes in life.

Now, let's look for clues that suggest to which guild-hall you might belong. For each question, we've included typical responses that someone might give. Your job is to rate the answers from 1 to 4. The one you like best is number 1. The one you like least is ranked number 4. All right, get a pen or pencil and create your country!

1. Where is your country?

Somewhere warm with gentle breezes   _____

Cool mountains, or it doesn't really matter   _____

Somewhere exciting, new, and different
where no one has ever been before   _____

A familiar place   _____

2. What is the topography?

Comfortable, easy, and nice   _____

Challenging with areas to conquer   _____

Varied with different and interesting areas   _____

Terrain similar to where you live now   _____

3. What is the climate?

Warm   _____

Cold, or doesn't matter   _____

Changing from day to day   _____

Familiar (as in seasonal)   _____

4. What is your government's philosophy?

Generous (takes care of the citizens)   _____

Capitalistic (competitive economy)   _____

Laissez-faire or experimental   _____

Cautiously traditional and solid   _____

5. What is your national product, if any?

Hospitality, tourism, or things such as a
health care center of excellence   _____

Whatever will sell and make a profit   _____

Experimental and new technology on
the cutting edge   _____

Products you can rely on to always work,
things you've dealt with in the past   _____

6. Which statement best reflects your international relations?

Peaceful international relations   _____

Focused on trade agreements   _____

Usually not important unless it opens up
new areas to explore   _____

Traditional, longstanding alliances   _____

7. What do you use for transportation?

Something familiar   _____

Something new or experimental   _____

Something efficient   _____

Horses, bicycles, walking, and/or
restored vehicles   _____

8. What do you do with your aged and infirm?

Take care of them at home   _____

Something efficient that works   _____

Doesn't matter, not an issue unless we
can create a newer, better way   _____

Something safe, acceptable, reasonable,
secure, and tested by experience   _____

All right, it's time to score yourself. For now, ignore question number 7. For all the others, go through and place the letter "H" beside the first line, "C" beside the second line, "E" beside the third line, and "M" beside the fourth line. For question number 7, mark the letters in backward, so from top down they'll read M, E, C, H. Now, add up your score for each letter. Your lowest score will tell you your guildhall: H is the Helper's Guildhall, C is the Challengers', E is the Explorers' and M is the Maintainers'.

Assuming you're following instructions and taking this test before reading the book (*Good for you!*), you'll be glad to know that each of these four names will have meaning for you once you've read the book. If you've got a tie score, then we suggest you go to the Internet, where a much more sophisticated mathematical formula will tell you your role in response to eight multiple-choice questions. If you can't access the Internet, don't worry. You may have a tie, but once you have read *Kingdomality* you'll have no trouble deciding which of the two guildhalls is most appealing.

Now, flip back to the front of the book and join us on a Kingdomality journey.

ACKNOWLEDGMENTS

SERVICES AVAILABLE

Sheldon Bowles, Richard Silvano, and Susan Silvano speak to conventions and organizations all over the world. Their messages are available on audio and video.

Extensive training and team-building programs based on Kingdomality are available, as well as seminars, workshops, and train-the-trainer certification programs.

For further information on Kingdomality programs, please contact the Kingdomality desk at

Career Management International
235 West 18th Street
Houston, TX 77008
(800) 426-7345
(713) 623-4569
www.careermanagement.com

Career Management International, Inc. provides human resource services, including outplacement, relocation counseling and move management, management interventions and career coaching, career alignment, strategic workforce planning, diversity training, and team building. CMI recognizes the substantial investment that corporations make in human capital and delivers effective programs required by businesses to maximize the return on that investment.

For information about having Sheldon Bowles speak to your organization, please contact

Ode To Joy Limited
165 Kennedy Street
Suite 5
Winnepeg, MB R3C 1S6
(204) 943-6642
www.sheldonbowles.com